My
Conversations
with **MARTIN LUTHER**

My
Conversations
with **MARTIN LUTHER**

*in which I learn about God,
faith, marriage, sexuality,
family, education, war,
spirituality, church
life, the future,
ecumenism, politics,
heaven, and other
things, too.*

TIMOTHY F. LULL

Augsburg
MINNEAPOLIS

To the Lutherans of New England
"My grace is sufficient for you, for my power is
made perfect in weakness."

—2 Corinthians 12:9

MY CONVERSATIONS WITH MARTIN LUTHER
In Which I Learn About God, Faith, Marriage, Sexuality, Family, Education,
War, Spirituality, Church Life, the Future, Ecumenism, Politics, Heaven, and
Other Things, Too

Book design by Timothy W. Larson
Cover design by Lecy Design

Library of Congress Cataloging-in-Publication Data
Lull, Timothy F.
  My conversations with Martin Luther : in which I learn about God, faith, mar-
riage, sexuality, family, education, war, spirituality, church life, the future, ecu-
menism, politics, heaven, and other things, too / Timothy F. Lull.
    p. cm.
  Includes bibliographical references.
  ISBN 0-8066-3898-2 (alk. paper)
  1. Lutheran Church—Doctrines. 2. Imaginary conversations. I. Title.
BX8065.2 .L85 1999
230'.41—dc21   99-28310
                                                              CIP

The paper used in this publication meets the minimum requirements of American National Standard for Information Sciences—Permanence of Paper for
Printed Library Materials, ANSI Z329.48-1984.

Manufactured in the U.S.A.   AF 9-3898

03   02   01   00   99   2   3   4   5   6   7   8   9   10

CONTENTS

PREFACE
FOUR WORDS TO THE READER

I have four things to say to the reader of this book before he or she begins. The first is a word of apology. Had I known that I was going to have continuing conversations with Dr. Martin Luther, I would have taken more careful notes from the beginning. As it is, I've kept a good record beginning with the second visit. My memory of all five of these conversations is vivid, and I hope that I have been a good reporter of my experience, even some years after the fact. (Once I sensed the visits might continue, I began to take careful notes just after Luther left, but always felt constrained not to write anything down in Dr. Luther's presence. So even here I may be filtering things just slightly.)

The second thing is to acknowledge that many readers will be skeptical that these conversations ever took place, except in my own imagination. They are entitled to their opinion. But I believe the book will make for better reading if those who decide to explore it will put away such questions as what did and did not happen, what might or might not have taken place, and instead follow what Dr. Luther has to say—whether from any actual visit or in my (supposed) fantasy.

The third is a word of regret for Luther's writings on the Jews, especially those from the 1540s, and of commiseration with any readers who are shocked by learning about these things for the first time. These are a great blot on Luther's achievements, and I think the text of this book will make that clear. To help clarify their negative status for contemporary Lutherans, I've attached as an appendix the 1994 Statement of the Church Council of the ELCA to the Jewish People repudiating the views that Luther expressed.

The final word is one of hope—that Luther will become for my readers, as he has for me, a living voice, a conversation partner about the gospel and the church in our situation today. In almost thirty years of teaching, this has been one abiding passion for me: to get people to take Luther off the shelf, to read him (rather than read about him), and to ponder his proposals about how to speak of God and what it means to be the church.

So the best upshot of this book would be if you were encouraged to have your own conversations with Martin Luther. I can't predict whether or not he'll pay you a visit, but I have written these pages and added suggestions for further reading with the lively hope that soon you will be visiting with Luther yourself. I predict that he won't tell you what to do in a simple sense (any more than he answered directly my most pointed questions about what should happen in the church today), but you will find these visits rewarding and eventually so indispensable that you'll be talking with Luther about things that really matter whether or not he comes to visit. It's habit-forming, and some habits are good for us.

The First Visit
Berkeley, Calif., October 1989

I'm tempted to begin the report of my first meeting with Martin Luther by saying that "it was a dark and stormy night." I won't say that because I know that many readers would shut the book immediately, and because I can't remember whether or not the night was stormy—at least until Luther's arrival. It certainly was dark, and I can remember that clearly because I walked the quarter mile from our house uphill to my office at Pacific Lutheran Theological Seminary in Berkeley with a flashlight in my hand. Deer from the nearby park roam around our campus at night. Many of them are very large—and on the whole you hope they see you coming a long way off, so that you don't run into a young buck on a narrow path. I saw no deer that night, but the owls that live in the tall trees near the office were making their repeated, low sounds.

It was late in October of 1989. I remember that because I was on my way to my office to work on a lecture and a sermon for Reformation Sunday, which was coming very soon. We had just moved to California a few weeks before and had already experienced our first earthquake, the very destructive *temblor* that will always be remembered for interrupting the World Series that year. For all that, I was excited to be living in the wonderful San Francisco area, stimulated by my new position as Academic Dean at the seminary, and very proud of my newly published anthology *Martin Luther's Basic Theological Writings*. Now that I had a "Luther book" out, I was eager to do an especially good job in my Reformation presentations.

I don't know how long I had worked when I became aware of the presence of Dr. Luther in the room. Let me explain at the outset that I always called him "Dr. Luther" and he always called me "Lull" in all our conversations. That seemed natural from the first moment. So when I looked up, I found myself more amazed than frightened, saying to my visitor, "Dr. Luther, what a surprise to see you!"

I don't suppose that you'll have any trouble understanding that I knew that it was Luther and not some other spirit of the past; he is always quite recognizable in a group picture. If anything surprised me about his physical appearance, it was that he looked like pictures of Luther in his younger years (at about age forty—that is, very vigorous and rather handsome). Perhaps eternal life has a pleasant surprise for all of us in this respect, but that's a question we never explored in his visits. He was wearing a robe of some sort, but I'm not enough of an expert on late-medieval costume to know whether it was a monk's robe or a doctoral robe. His voice was considerably higher than I might have expected for a large man, but not squeaky or unpleasant. His English was without German accent, but with a slight British, rather than American, quality.

"Well, Lull," he replied, "I've been wanting to talk to you for the last few weeks, and this seemed a good occasion. Do you have a little time to visit with me? I don't want to keep you from your work." These sentences made me uneasy in a way that his cheerful appearance alone had not. I began to sense—quite rightly—that Luther was going to be asking me some questions. The old knot in my stomach from defending my doctoral dissertation returned for the first time in many years. But Luther talked on in such a cheery way that I was quickly at ease again.

Copies of my newly published book were sitting on one corner of the desk. Luther picked one up and began to look through it. I thought he smiled at the cover, which has a very handsome portrait of him by his artist friend Lucas Cranach. He spent some time looking at the mechanical aspects of printing—the binding and the paper stock. He mumbled a few approving comments but then looked up and came to the point: "Yes, this new edition of my writings, Lull, this is the very thing that I wanted to discuss with you. So you had the courage to edit me?"

Suddenly I understood the occasion for the visit. Luther continues to be interested in his reputation, his reception by later generations. Luther needs editing; I think even he would agree with that. The English-language edition of his basic works, which contains only a part of his total output in Latin and German, runs to fifty-five volumes. I began to explain that this was a major reason for my undertaking the task of boiling all that Luther down to a single volume. I had been a teacher for some years and wanted my students to have access to writings of Luther that were scattered in more separate volumes than they could afford to buy.

"Very considerate for those students," remarked Luther, and I could imagine that we might have veered off into tales of how easy things were for students today in comparison to the 16th century. But Luther pressed a little more. "This has been a lot of work for you. You have neglected your own writing to make one more 'Luther book.' Aren't there enough already?"

I remembered how often Luther had said in his own lifetime that he feared that his writings (and those of his colleagues such as Philipp Melanchthon) would keep people from reading the Bible, rather than help them to read it correctly. So I knew that we were on dangerous ground. I explained that in recent decades people had more often read about Luther than read Luther himself. When Luther pressed me on the reason for this, I stressed that some of the current biographies and studies are very good (which is true). I did not mention that many people find Luther either offensive in some of his views or so easily distracted that he wanders quickly from the point.

"Well, you haven't done badly, Lull," he remarked, and I breathed such a clear sigh of relief that he laughed out loud. "But where is my commentary on the Magnificat? I heard that you had planned to include that, but I don't find it here in the published edition." Luther was right. I had hoped to include that wonderful writing from his time in the Wartburg Castle. It shows the tender regard with which Luther always spoke of the Mother of our Lord (a great shock to some subsequent Lutherans who came to assume that to be Lutheran was to do or think the opposite of the Roman Catholics on every issue). It also is a wonderful piece of Luther's own theology, for he finds in Mary's Son the true pattern of the hidden and surprising ways of God, who is always casting down the mighty from their thrones and lifting up the lowly.

But how was I going to explain the reason that this document had been omitted? To understand this I feared I would have to go into the whole sad history of the various Lutheran groups in the United States, who jointly published Luther's works in those fifty-five volumes some decades ago, but now do very little cooperatively. I began to explain legal matters to. him, "You see, Dr. Luther, the publishing rights to the Magnificat in English belong to the Concordia Publishing House of the Lutheran Church Missouri Synod. . . ."

At that point Luther interrupted with his hand held up: "Say no more, Lull; I can well imagine that those who bear my name—a strange business in itself—and call themselves Lutherans have me so chopped up that I have to be edited in competing volumes." I lowered my head because Luther had gone to the heart of the matter and there was nothing else to say on that front.

Luther brought things back to a positive note by asking which of the writings were my personal favorites. This gave us a chance to talk at length about his writings, a mutually enjoyable enterprise since authors generally love to discuss their works, and editors wonder whether they have done well by the author on whose material they have been working. So I told Luther how much I loved his *Small Catechism*. I reported that there had been a struggle with the publishers about including it, as it was so widely available. But I convinced them that this wonderful summary of basic Christian teaching was even more interesting when read with its preface, in which Luther describes the deplorable conditions among churches in the countryside that led to the writing of this little gem.

Luther beamed with satisfaction and noted that of all his writings, this one had probably been the most widely known down through the centuries, by Lutherans and non-Lutherans alike. I remarked very carefully that the catechism is very positive in tone, that it does not include the quarrels among the various parties, which are so predominant in Luther's other writings.

"I make no apology for what you call 'quarrels,' Lull," he replied. "We were fighting hard for the gospel not only against the power of the Roman church, but against many who wanted to make it an occasion for disorder or personal self-indulgence. But when it was time to write a basic account of the faith for beginners, something that could be used in the home and in the humblest local parish, we knew that the 'quarrels' did not belong at that point."

"But the *Small Catechism* is a very safe choice, Lull," continued Luther. "Which of my other writings do you especially enjoy?" He seemed to sense that it was perhaps not quite appropriate for a writer to pump a reader for compliments, but I was thinking hard of which to choose—I admired so many documents. So I didn't really mind being questioned along these lines.

"Your writings on the interpretation of Scripture are very simple, very powerful, very helpful with our struggles in the church today," I reported. I told him how my students were regularly shocked at the "freedom" with which he seemed to approach the Bible. "They are amazed that you value some books more than others—the so-called 'canon within the canon.'"

"Who can take all that Bible equally seriously?" asked Luther sharply. "That is the road to madness. Of course, all Scripture is written for our instruction, and all of it ought to be considered over the year in preaching or perhaps—in the case of some of the harder books—in teaching. But I continue to love best those books that point most strongly to the gospel, especially Paul's letters and the Gospel of John. I will admit that I've changed my mind about some matters thanks to the remedial Bible study that I've been doing in heaven."

I was shocked that the great Dr. Martin Luther would have to do "remedial Bible study." It made me tremble for what this might imply the assignments in eternity will be for the rest of us. Luther was enjoying the shock value of what he had shared with me, but he went on to explain that he had been working over some centuries to come to a better understanding of the Epistle of James.

"That's the book that you called 'an epistle of straw,'" I commented. "You said that it has 'nothing of the nature of the gospel about it.'[1] And yet you have to spend centuries in study to come to better understanding? Perhaps you were wrong about faith and works after all!"

Luther bristled and I realized that I had spoken too strongly—perhaps caused by this surprising turn of the conversation. "No, Lull," he answered very slowly, "that wasn't the problem. What I missed in James was something else altogether. The problem was my lack of attention to James 3. You do remember what James 3 is about, don't you Lull?"

Now I was squirming, and Luther seemed to be enjoying that for a moment, but then he took a Bible off the shelf and handed it to me, saying, "Take and read." So I read the opening verses of the chapter:

> Not many of you should become teachers, my brothers and sisters, for you know that we who teach will be judged with greater strictness. For all of us make many mistakes. Anyone who makes no mistakes in speaking is perfect, able to keep the whole body in check with a bridle. (James 3:1-2 NRSV)

Luther was becoming impatient. "Skip ahead a little. I can't tell whether you understand or not." So I began reading from a little later in the chapter:

> How great a forest is set ablaze by a small fire! And the tongue is a fire. The tongue is placed among our members as a world of iniquity; it stains the whole body, sets on fire the cycle of nature, and is itself set on fire by hell. (James 3:5-6)

Now I thought I understood, but Luther spoke very quietly to be sure that I had not missed the point. His great downfall, at crucial points in the Reformation, had been his own inability to restrain his tongue. His great gift of articulate and powerful speech could be fatefully misused to call down violent destruction on the peasants during the rebellion of 1525 or to curse the Jews in the writings at the end of his life.[2]

Now I was very quiet, wanting to ask a thousand questions but sensing that Dr. Luther had said all that he would say on this subject. Luther himself broke the silence by saying, "You read well from the Scriptures, but I always find American accents so very shocking." I complimented him on his very fine command of English and asked how he had come to learn it.

"You might think there is nothing to do in eternity," replied Luther, "but you would be wrong, Lull. I learned English so that I could read the plays of William Shakespeare, which I find especially interesting. There isn't much else in your language that I need, but it is worth the trouble for this one great writer."

I asked whether he had a favorite Shakespeare play, and I should not have been surprised at his answer, which was *Hamlet*.

"You will think," said Luther, "that my attraction is to the fact that the Prince of Denmark has been a student at Wittenberg University at the beginning of the play. And that was my original interest when Melanchthon showed this play to me. But as I got caught up in the great power of the writer, I came to appreciate the drama for quite another reason. It has to do with a theological point, Lull. Can you guess what it is?"

"Does it have something to do with the ghost?" I asked, guessing wildly, and perhaps influenced by the fact that I seemed to be entertaining a ghost myself.

"Yes, exactly," Luther replied. "The real point of the play to me is that Hamlet cannot ever tell with complete certainty whether the shade that purports to be his Father is actually a ghost or is in fact the devil, full of lies and misleading, tragic suggestions as always. By the end of the play, we think that the ghost has been truthful, and that Claudius has murdered his brother. But we can never be completely sure. This and the fine, deep speeches are the things I admire most about *Hamlet*."

"But Dr. Luther," I replied urgently. "That raises a real question about this conversation we are having. How can I be sure that I am talking to you, and not to the devil purporting to be you, using disguise and trickery to mislead me?"

"Now that's a wonderful question!" exclaimed Luther. "It's worthy of a theologian, which is what I understand that you are. A professor of systematic theology, is that what they call you? Well, I tell you, Lull, too many theologians today assume that any experience, especially a powerful one, is necessarily valid and true. Your age understands many things that we did not comprehend 500 years ago, but on this point I think we were a little wiser. You will have to wait and see whether our conversation tonight is reliable and true, when compared to things that you can trust far more than a midnight visitor, like the Word of God itself."

There was silence for a minute while we both considered all of this, and then I got my courage up to ask, "Didn't your father suggest that it might have been the prompting of the devil that led you to enter the monastery in 1505?"

Luther laughed. "Yes, Hans Luther had a pretty good theology himself," he explained, "even though he had no formal education. But I was so mad at that suggestion that it put a strain on my relationship with my father for years. Only much later, in 1521, could I write to him and say that perhaps he had been right all along. Although I only say 'perhaps,' because I can't imagine that I could have fulfilled my vocation without the long detour through the Augustinian order."[3]

This led me to ask Luther, again with some delicacy, whether he ever changed his mind. At first the question puzzled him, and he asked me to say more of what I meant. "People today think of you as a person of great conviction, one who was steadfast under pressure, perhaps even, by modern standards, somewhat stubborn. So the question arises—did you, once arriving at your original theological insight, ever change your mind?"

"Have you been to my Wittenberg?" Luther asked. At that time I had not, but I told him of my wish to go. (The Berlin Wall would come down just the next month after this conversation, making travel in Luther's parts of Germany much easier in years to come.) "You'll see that they've made me quite a Prussian," he chuckled. "All of this stern 'Here I Stand' business, and the Castle Church almost transformed into a monument to German nationalism. It's disgusting. But I see what you mean. I was steadfast and resolute about some issues throughout my career—the deadly seriousness of our bondage to sin, for example. I was very firm with the Swiss at Marburg about the Lord's Supper, and I've never come to regret that, even though I'd admit that all the centuries of division that followed from it were not necessarily for the best.

"But on many issues, I had to change my mind as I thought more deeply about a question or had to consider the pastoral consequences. I was far too reckless about the role of faith in the sacraments early on, and I came to realize that I was in danger of making the human response on a par with or even greater than the promise of the Word. Or take questions of war and peace. You can read whole shelves in libraries about how my so-called political views changed over the years. Most of this is well meant but pretty funny, because these books approach the question as if I had been a detached philosopher rather than a person trying to help the churches and my princes in the midst of confusing events."

"Have you changed your mind about any questions now that you are in eternity?" I asked, perhaps rather recklessly.

"Your question betrays a very simplistic view of how things are there, and that is not the real point of my visit," said Luther. "The first thing that happens is a great relaxation of the impulse to think that you are in charge of the universe. Of course we always ought to let God be God, but in heaven there is little choice. I still think about many things, and laugh about some while I grumble about others, and I still study, as you have learned in our conversation tonight. But all of this must be done in a very low key, in a very small voice, knowing that all these matters are wisely being worked out in the hands of our gracious Lord."

Now I was very silent. I realized the impertinence of my remark and felt that instead of receiving a rebuke, Luther had pulled the curtain back for me for just a minute to give me a glimpse of that peace which passes human understanding, even for persons as important and intense as the Reformer. But he wasn't done with the subject.

"Having said that, Lull, I'm curious what you were wondering about. On which question did you want information about whether I had changed my mind?"

"The ordination of women," I quickly answered. In editing the anthology, I had decided not to edit out Luther's very negative comments on the subject, in his 1539 treatise, "On the Councils and the Church." There he had written about the pastoral office:

> It is, however, true that the Holy Spirit has excepted women, children, and incompetent people from this function, but chooses (except in emergencies) only competent males to fill this office, as one reads here and there in the epistles of St. Paul that a bishop must be pious, able to teach, and the husband of one wife—and in I Corinthians 14 he says, "The women should keep silence in the churches." In summary, it must be a competent and chosen man.[4]

Luther paused for what seemed a long time, then said, "Yes, I see what you mean. You've ordered the church in your time in quite a different way than what seemed the only possibility to me. Now you ask whether it is all right to have done so. Except I don't think you really ask, because I sense, Lull, that this is a test, and you are pretty well convinced of the rightness of what your church—this interesting church that bears my name—has done."

I was sweating, but Luther went on, very calmly and with increasing warmth. "Who am I that you should come to me for permission on such a question? Am I your pope, with the disadvantage of being dead and therefore only rarely able to be consulted? No, this is no affair of mine. You are on your own here, as you really know, and Martin Luther will neither bless nor condemn this decision."

He saw that I looked disappointed. "All right," he continued, "since I assume you do understand what I've just said, I'll say a little more. How did I respond when I heard about this development? I must admit that I was surprised and not a little agitated.

"The peace of eternity comes upon us slowly, even in the great light of that place. So I fussed a bit, rather quietly, of course, and then I started to laugh at the thought of how it would have vexed my old adversary Leo X and all the popes who came after him if I had not only married Katie, but made her a pastor in the bargain. She would have been quite good, I think, for in some ways she was better suited for that task than I was.

"So I can see why you've done what you've done and I have learned to laugh about it—good, hearty laughter that is almost a blessing. But I want to be sure that you understand that we can only have these conversations if you understand that I cannot solve your problems for you, as if Luther were the new Moses, the legislator on all questions before the church."

I'm rather sure he spoke of "conversations," but I did not pay special attention to that at the time, since I assumed that his visit was a onetime event, caused by his desire to discuss the new edition of his writings that I had published. And when almost ten years passed before I saw Dr. Luther again, you can understand why I thought the conversation reported here was my one opportunity.

I'm afraid that I must admit that I don't recall all that we talked about on that long, dark evening, and I may not have the events in exactly the right order. I know we came back after a time to the question of the Bible, and that Luther did complain about what seemed to him the relative neglect of the Bible in "his churches," at least in the United States of America.

"The women are the only ones who really do much Bible study," he exclaimed, "unless I have witnessed it incorrectly." I told him that he was surely right about this, but that even the Women's Bible Studies were in danger of being swept away by the busyness of life in our day.

"You will pay a high price for that busyness," scowled Luther, "but I don't think that's the only problem. Your own pastors seem somewhat reluctant to lead at this point. In comparison to our day, your graduates have years and years of education, but when they take up parish service they seem like Martha to be 'busy with many things.' And the preaching! I hear everything but the

Word, and what little there is comes more as milk for newborns than solid food."

I spent some time somewhat unsuccessfully trying to explain this in terms of Bible study: our churches were quite concerned to distinguish themselves from the fundamentalists, the evangelicals, and others who make a great emphasis on the authority of Scripture.

Luther brushed all this aside. "I have said that I cannot give you advice on how to solve your dilemmas," he continued, "and that is true. But I can tell you when things are not right. You are living in a time when Christians get very little encouragement for their faith at work, in the community, even sometimes at home. That is hard for you, and yet it could also be an opportunity if you did a better job of setting your priorities. My colleagues and I worked hard to make the Bible available in the language of the people for our day, but if the people will not read it and their pastors will not encourage them, how can the church be faithful, especially when you are surrounded by so many different religions and such general comfort that most people become quite content with their lives and very indifferent about their faith?"

I thought Luther was beginning to sound a bit like Søren Kierkegaard, the 19th-century Danish theologian and philosopher who made a powerful critique of the flat and listless Christianity of his day.[5] I asked Luther whether he knew Kierkegaard.

"Lull," he replied, "I know him. He's quite a boy, not at all afraid of what you call 'quarrels' with your exaggerated love of peace and harmony. We've gone at it a few times, and we have much yet to discuss and all the time in the world in which to get around to it. Perhaps you will understand that for the first few hundred years that one lives in eternity, one is busy touching base with people from one's own era—not only family and friends, but even coming to see old adversaries in a new way in the bright, clear light of that city that needs no lamp for its illumination."

I sensed that the end of the visit was near as Luther rose and began to pace around the room. He glanced at a few books, but did not say anything. I was very much caught up in thinking about all that we had discussed. But he wasn't quite finished, "So, Lull," he continued, "what is your greatest hope for your book and how reading my old writings might help people today?"

I had thought about that and had an answer ready. "You've been a powerful continuing teacher for us, Dr. Luther, because your work is about one thing, and yet about many." Luther looked at me intently, and I continued. "You are a one-issue theologian, and the one issue is the gospel. This is what humans need in every time and in every place. And yet you put the gospel before us in its several forms—as the surprise of justification by grace, freely, and for Christ's sake, as the paradox of Christian freedom, in which we find our destiny and genuine freedom by forgetting ourselves and serving others. You teach us that while the gospel is simple, in God's great imagination it comes to us in many ways—in the Word, in baptism, in the Supper, in confession and forgiveness, in mutual consolation of brother and sisters—each of which reinforces the others and any one of which may be the word of power for a given person at a given time.

"But what I find most helpful of all for our time, Dr. Luther, is your theology of the cross, at least as I understand it."

"And how do you understand it, Lull?" he asked.

Luther's theology of the cross is something that I lecture about often. I fear I started out a little too professorially: "In your time you were fighting the false confidence that reason could help humans define God, understand God, even find their way to God. Your theology of the cross made room for the mystery again, for the gift-character of the gospel, which comes not as the fulfillment of our brightest and best moments, but as a surprise, as sheer experience of grace, often where and when we least expect it.

Luther was laughing before I could stop myself. "Well, Lull," he said, "that was just great, but a pretty big load to dump on a late-night visitor. I've heard you can really get going when you want to. But don't take my laughter the wrong way; it was also because you actually have read me well. What you say about the gospel as a gift and a surprise does gladden my heart."

"Thank you," I said, thinking that going on any longer would be a mistake.

But Luther pressed me. "How is it in your time, Lull? Do people still have false confidence in reason?"

So I continued, but a bit more slowly. I told how some value science by thinking of it as providing all the answers, all certainty. Others are quite discouraged about reason having any role to play at all—both Christians and those outside the church. I told how they turn to astrology, occult practices, or whatever else can be found to bring the mystery back into life.

"Oh," said Luther, looking quite unhappy, "astrology won't help. Melanchthon was into that, but I've always thought it was all hogwash. No, the mystery itself comes as a gift. You can no more bring it back by trying hard than you can banish it by your best professional efforts. The cross judges all—both human pride in reason but also our despair. What do you say about the cross to your students? Tell me more, Lull."

So I went on one more time, hesitant to say too much, but eager for either confirmation or correction. "Dr. Luther, what we've learned from you above all is to expect to be prepared to be surprised by God. That's where the cross confounds us still. If such a terrible event is the high point of God's love and mercy for the world, then how can we know what comes next? We have to hang easy about both our success and our failures. We are forced to go forward along our life ways, knowing that we are not the final judges of how we are doing, what is really happening, or how it all will turn out."

"Good, good," said Luther, "even very good. You do also mention the forgiveness of sins, I trust."

I nodded, astonished and embarrassed to have said so much. Luther put me quickly at ease. "Not bad, Lull. You have some real promise. You are on the right track. Keep teaching along these lines, and especially keep digging in the Word of God, and you will be helpful to the church in your time."

I don't think I've had a higher affirmation of my calling as a pastor and teacher in the church. But Luther was headed for the door, and I wanted one last thing, if he would be willing. So I quickly asked, "Dr. Luther, would you read one passage for me, one that I especially love, about the work of a theologian?"

Luther stopped and turned around, smiled and

said, "I know just what you mean, I think, and since it's late at night, I'll even read you some Luther in English, although I don't like the way I sound." So he picked up the anthology, opened to a passage that he quickly found, and read:

> If, however, you feel that are inclined to think you have made it, flattering yourself with your own little books, teaching, or writing, because you have done it beautifully and preached excellently; if you are highly pleased when someone praises you in the presence of others; if you perhaps look for praise, and would sulk or quit what you are doing if you did not get it— if you are of that stripe, dear friend, then take yourself by the ears, and if you do this in the right way you will find a beautiful pair of big, long, shaggy donkey ears. Then do not spare any expense! Decorate them with golden bells, so that people will be able to hear you wherever you go, point their fingers at you, and say, "See, See! There goes that clever beast, who can right such exquisite books and preach so remarkably well."[6]

And then Dr. Luther was gone. I've had occasion since that visit to keep studying Luther. I think I know where the problems are in Luther's theology, and the worst of them "cause me to tremble," in the words of the old spiritual. But I think I keep coming back for more because there is something right about a Christian—with such great gifts and such great flaws—who can so effectively laugh at himself.

The Second Visit
Berkeley, Calif., May 1998

Almost a decade passed after my first visit with
Luther. At times I might have wondered whether
it really happened, had not the memory of it been
such a powerful stimulus to further study. I realized in a vivid way what I've always been trying to
tell my students—that each reading of an author
is the opportunity for a conversation.

There were changes in my life during these
years. I moved from the dark, cozy basement
office where I had talked with Luther to a bright
clean space overlooking the San Francisco Bay. I
visited Germany in 1996, and had occasion to see
for the first time so many of the places that were
important in Luther's life. But there were no
visions, no conversations, no direct encounters at
Luther's monastery in Erfurt, in Wittenberg, or at
the Wartburg Castle.

That same fall I was elected President of Pacific
Lutheran Theological Seminary. Our family
moved up the hill into the President's Residence,
and I moved my office yet again—now to a lovely
room also overlooking the Bay, but directly above

the basement office where I had talked with Luther some years earlier.

The winter of 1997–98 was very severe in the San Francisco area. We don't have snow and ice, of course, but we had record rain and wind. In early February I had to come back from a speaking tour in the Northwest (where I had been lecturing on Luther's understanding of the church as community) because of a potential disaster. Our school, built on a beautiful hill overlooking Berkeley, San Francisco, and the Golden Gate Bridge, was experiencing terrible mudslides. We were in danger of losing the road that connects the upper and the lower parts of our campus.

By the time I flew home from Portland, the crisis seemed under control. Our students and the city of Berkeley worked together to spread plastic across the hill. The road held and the mudslides stopped. I thanked those who had worked and prepared to raise money for the repair of the hillside (it eventually cost more than $250,000) and, hopeful that the danger was past, I flew to Chicago to give a speech.

The next day I called home just to be sure that everything was all right. When my son said, "You'd better talk to Mom," I knew something was wrong. I learned that a windstorm had blown the top third of a Monterey Pine crashing into my office. The tree came through the ceiling in two places (with water pouring in all over the contents). In another place the tree pushed through the outside wall, smashing a bookcase that had been bolted to the wall down onto my desk. Volumes of Luther's Works went flying across the office like a barrage of missiles.

Once again students came to the rescue, helping our business manager and my wife pull books, papers, computers, and photographs out of the office. By the time I got home, the holes in the wall were covered with plastic and everything was beginning to dry out. I quickly saw two things: that even more repairs would be necessary and—even more disturbing—that if I had been sitting at my desk I would probably have been killed, either by the crashing bookcase or by the impact on my head of flying volumes of Martin Luther.

Some months passed. The life of a seminary goes on—disasters or not. In fact, the accreditation team came to review us the next week. The workmen started their repairs. The office was soon back to an even more beautiful state than before, as a wonderful hardwood floor was discovered under the wet carpet. When I moved back in, I moved the furniture so that my back would face an inside wall. Several other large trees had been cut down, but I didn't want to take any chances.

Holy Week and Easter passed. It was soon to be the season of synod assemblies when seminary presidents travel to thank the folks who send money for our support. I was preparing a series of lectures for the Southwestern Washington Synod in Tacoma. I believe that Bishop Wold had suggested that I might "do something with Luther" in one of my presentations.

And then, on that warm spring night, I had my second visit from Martin Luther. I was aware of his presence in my office for several minutes before he spoke. He seemed to be inspecting the new walls, the repairs to the balcony and the ceiling, and to be looking carefully—as he had done before—at my books. Then he began to chuckle, in his always surprisingly high voice. "Well, Lull," he said, "I see you no longer have my volumes behind your back."

I hadn't thought about it, but of course the rearrangement of the office led to a different ordering of the books. I now had my biblical books behind me, with Luther off a little to one side. He continued to chuckle. "But if the devil pushes those shelves over again, I suspect that some big volume like *Biblical Theology of the Old and New Testaments* can be just as deadly for you as any of my works."[1]

"Hello, Dr. Luther," I said. "I'm really glad but quite surprised to see you again. I wasn't counting on another visit."

"You can imagine, Lull," he continued, "that I have lots of work to do in heaven. And in my free time, lots of visits to make here on earth. And I do try to save some time for making music. I thought we had settled things rather nicely last time I was here. You seemed well set in your work as a theologian. But I when I heard that you had almost been killed by flying copies of my works, I had to come see this for myself."

Something was irritating me in his approach. I was, of course, very honored to see him again, to think that he might stay long enough for another visit. But all this smiling, laughing, and chuckling about my near miss was getting on my nerves. "I guess I can see the funny side of it," I countered. "But I'm not yet laughing about it. Not by a long shot. I really begin to shake when I think what could have happened."

"Of course you do, Lull," he replied, "and that's good for you, though you modern people don't like to have that pointed out. I don't understand everything about your time, and certainly little about your problems, but it seems to me that you all go on as if death is only a theoretical possibility or a distant reality. If we had lost our nerve at every close call in my day, we would never have gotten any work done at all."

"Do you have any advice for overcoming this kind of scare?" I asked, now genuinely interested in his approach and somewhat less irritated.

"The Psalms are best for this kind of thing," replied Luther. "In them we find a few people carefree and full of praise and thanksgiving. But most of the speakers are in trouble, needing rescue or forgiveness, even surrounded by their enemies.

I don't want to say that a close call is a good thing. But God can bring good out of it, if you consider your situation in the mirror of the Word." And he especially recommended Psalm 57:1 (NRSV):

> *Be merciful to me, O God, be merciful to me,*
> *for in you my soul takes refuge;*
> *in the shadow of your wings I will take refuge,*
> *until the destroying storms pass by.*

The mention of the Bible reminded me of Luther's astonishing news on his earlier visit that he had been engaged in remedial Bible study— study of the book of James, about which he had said some rather dismissive things.[2] So I asked him how this was going.

"I've finished my work on James," said Luther with great satisfaction, "and perhaps I've even learned to curb my tongue a bit. You can judge that for yourself in this conversation. So I've moved on to my next assignment." He paused and saw the surprise on my face that from such a great biblical scholar even more remedial Bible study would be required. "I'm now required to work on one of my old personal favorites—Paul's letter to the Romans."

If I had been amazed at his earlier report, this one was ever harder to accept. "Romans?" I stammered. "But you wrote the book on Romans. Your commentary is one of the great classics of the Christian church."

"Thank you, I'm sure," Luther replied, "but that's not quite the whole story. I don't think you can quite imagine how inadequate all our efforts are from the standpoint of eternity. The part of Romans that I am assigned currently is chapters 9–11, about the Jews and their apparent refusal to accept Christ. I am beginning to see that I didn't quite hear Paul correctly on this subject. Read me that verse from chapter 11 about God not going back on his promises."

I grabbed my Bible off the shelf—the New Revised Standard Version, which I always have at hand. I suppose it would have been very classy to grab the Luther Bible and read the verse in German, but I was not quick enough to think of that. Instead I read the requested verse in English: "For the gifts and the calling of God are irrevocable" (Romans 11:29).

"I'm afraid," admitted Luther, "that I did not quite understand the Word of God on this point, but rushed to the conclusion that I had already reached about the subject. When I gave my early lectures on Romans, I did notice the strong promise in this verse, but I assumed it meant that the Jews would turn back to Christ in my lifetime. I came to think that if only the gospel were restored in the church, then this promise would be fulfilled. I took God's judgment into my own hands when that did not happen according to my timetable. I suspect you know that a great deal of harm and damage came from what I eventually wrote on this subject."[3]

I did know about that indeed. Perhaps the greatest liability for Luther and for Lutheranism today is the widespread knowledge of his late and angry writings toward the Jews. I would not have dared to raise the subject. We had both been silent for a minute or two. It seemed to me he was now finished with this topic, and I was reluctant to continue the conversation.

Finally, Luther broke the silence, saying, "It's a very hard topic, Lull. Very difficult for me even now. Perhaps some day we can discuss it at greater length." That pleased me very much and planted the first seed of hope that this might not be our last visit. So I moved us on.

"I would consider that conversation a great privilege," I said. "But let me ask you now, what is the method of your heavenly Bible study, Dr. Luther, do you work individually or in groups? Perhaps the apostle Paul lectures to you directly on what he meant to say."

"It's nothing like that, Lull," he said. "We study in groups of about a dozen. We help each other come to a better understanding of the Word of God. We call them twelve-million-step groups, because it takes a long time to explore the height, and the breadth, and the depth of God's word. But one thing we have in eternity is all the time we need."

"May I ask about your group, Dr. Luther?" I said, not sure what might be acceptable or intrusive on this topic.

"Generally you work with people from your own time period," said Luther, "or at least that's how it seems to me. I suppose that the perspective of eternity dawns only slowly. For now our questions and blind spots seem quite parallel. I currently study with several people whose names you would recognize. One is King Henry VIII of England. Another is Pope Leo X."

Luther saw my amazement but simply smiled. Leo X was Giovanni de Medici, a son of the great family of Florence, a wonderful patron of the arts, and above all the pope who condemned and excommunicated Luther. He was also the pope who awarded the title "Defender of the Faith" to the English King Henry VIII, who had published a blistering attack on Luther—"The Defense of the Seven Sacraments." But, of course, eventually Henry fell out with the Roman church and ended up outside the Roman church himself. Yet Henry was never a friend of Luther's, and they continued to squabble in dueling publications.

Imagine Luther, Leo X, and Henry VIII taking up Saint Paul's theology! I wondered how group Bible study, even with twelve million steps, went in such a group. I wondered what I might be assigned in eternity—where on earth to begin calculating all of the Bible that I still don't know. I pondered who might be assigned to my group of twelve.

"I suppose you are wondering how we get along," said Luther. "The truth of the matter is that Henry is a great fellow. We've long since talked out our differences and now like to make lute and harpsichord music together when we can find the time. He says I would have made a great Archbishop of Canterbury, but that's just the kind of thing that old enemies say to each other when they finally become friends."

"And what about Leo X?" I asked.

"Well, I still have some way to go there," said Luther. "I can see that we were worried about quite different things in our own time. We have been able to have a laugh that I would have dedicated a book called *The Freedom of a Christian* to him—as that was not exactly his view of what was needed in the church. And I've come to understand that anyone who supported Michelangelo had a keen eye for something that I largely neglected."[4]

Since Luther was speaking of key leaders of the Roman Catholic and Anglican churches, I asked for his views on ecumenism, especially the issues before our church today.

"You'll have to understand this, Lull," he replied. "I'm happy to talk with you about any of these matters, but I can't solve your problems for you. It just wouldn't be right. It would take away your responsibility, and even your freedom, to do what you must do according to conscience in your own time."

"I'm surprised to hear you speak of freedom, Dr. Luther," I answered. "You are famous for your treatise *The Freedom of a Christian* but even more famous for your writing *The Bondage of the Will.*"[5]

"Now, Lull," he answered, "you're a better theologian than that. It must be getting late for you to ask such a confused question. So listen. We are indeed unable to find God by our own free will; he must be found by his love and grace. If you really understand the gospel, you don't walk around wearing a badge saying, 'I found it.' There is nothing to make me change my mind on this point.

"But in matters within our competence, including the life of the church in each generation, we do have freedom and also responsibility. You can't just 'pass the buck,' as you Americans like to say, by citing some random remark by Dr. Luther or anyone else, as if that would take you off the hook for issues that you must settle."

"If I follow you," I continued, "then on some issues we might today act very differently than you did in your time."

"Of course," said Luther. "We have already discussed Romans 11 and how inadequate—no, worse than inadequate—my views were there. But there's another example closer to hand and very dear to you in which your church has gone quite a different direction than my explicit teaching."

"Are you thinking of the ordination of women?" I asked.

"Yes," replied Luther. "You remember our conversation about the subject last time?"

"I do," I stated, "and was glad to see that you had come to favor the practice."

"Well, now," said Luther slowly, "*favor* is a very strong word. I think it would be more accurate to say that I understand better why some of my successors have adopted it. I always counseled that one needs to study Scripture broadly, not just looking at a single verse on any topic. But I must say that I got stuck on passages such as 1 Corinthians 14:34-36 where Paul says that women must keep silent in church. But there are other places, even in Paul, that could point in a different direction."

"We've been very influenced by Galatians 3:28," I reported.

"Yes," said Luther, "I know that one too: 'There is no longer Jew or Greek, there is no longer slave or free, there is no longer male and female; for all of you are one in Christ Jesus' (NRSV). Yes, I see that might mean something different for you than it did for me. You can look in my commentaries and see, but I don't think I really paused to pay much attention to the 'neither male nor female part.'"[6]

"I've always thought," I continued, "that the mention of women as Paul's coworkers in Philippians 4 was a sign of a complex and fluid situation for ministry in the early church." Luther seemed not interested in continuing to explore my views.

"I think your mind is made up, Lull," he said, "and I've told you that I've learned to live with it. So let's move on to something that is more—as you say—fluid. What else can we talk about?"

"So what about ecumenism, Dr. Luther?" I asked, hoping for some good material to help with all those synod assembly speeches that I was soon to make. "Should we have agreed to this basic mutual affirmation about justification by faith with the Catholics?"

"That topic is so complex and—to me—so much fun," replied Luther, "that I sometimes wish I were still a professor to get into the debate. There are details that you want to be careful about. So I can't and I won't tell you what your church must do. But I will say this. On any given Sunday, from what I understand, the odds are about as good for the gospel to be rightly preached and the sacraments rightly administered in a Roman Catholic parish as in a Lutheran congregation. Do you agree?"

"I do," I answered, "but even so that's only partly a cause for rejoicing. The way you put it implies that the odds aren't all that great for our basic message to be at the heart of what happens in many of our own congregations."

"You said it, Lull," replied Luther with a big

laugh. "But look on the bright side. This confessional brand identity has often disappointed, even from the beginning. My followers when they were in their right minds never claimed to have a monopoly on the gospel or the truth.

"Let me tell you something else about these Catholics today," Luther continued. "They really like to sing 'A Mighty Fortress Is Our God.' If I'm visiting your part of the universe and I hear it being sung as I pass a church, these days I assume that church must be Roman—unless it happens to be the last Sunday in October. You've really squeezed your heritage off to one side."

I was thinking about this and suddenly sensed that Luther might soon be leaving. He rarely stayed still. So I asked if we could discuss some of the other questions before our church.

"Fire away, Lull," was his reply.

"What about full communion with the Episcopalians?" I asked. "That's the hard one before us just now."

"I've already told you I'm not going to tell you what to do, Lull," he answered. "But is there some aspect of this that you want to ask me about?"

"Well, sir," I continued, "what about bishops and this matter of the historic episcopate?"

"As for bishops," said Luther, "you should consider yourselves quite lucky—in all these churches. I wish you had known Albrecht of Mainz and some of the other characters that I had to put up with in my day. The weakest bishop you have now would have been a real ally of the gospel and defender of the Reformation in my time. That's why you can't build an automatic bridge from my century to yourself. Things change."

"So you don't think it a bad thing that we have bishops?" I asked—not my own question, but one that clearly haunts many Lutherans to this day.

"No," said Luther, "not at all. You know about my friend Amsdorf[7] and how I put a lot of energy into installing him as bishop in Naumberg and in trying to support him in his work. Of course it was almost impossible, given the church structures of that day. It didn't work very well. But the idea of a good shepherd to the scattered Christian communities is not only valid, but a necessary help in times of trouble."

"Aren't there dangers even today in churches where bishops have too much power?" I asked, continuing to voice the doubts that plague many.

"Of course," said Luther. "The Augsburg Confession, which I believe that you do still know something about, is pretty explicit about this in Article 28. But there is also a danger in churches where pastors have too much power, and in churches where laity—especially a certain small group of laity—have too much power. Our human weaknesses all show up in our life in the church, and no magic form of church structure will deliver us from them.

"But surely you must have something other than bishops to discuss at these synod meetings," Luther continued. "What are the other issues?"

"Many are upset about the sexual misconduct of our public officials," I reported. "What can be done about this?"

Luther sighed. "It isn't a new problem," he said very quietly, "and it isn't a small one. I had a very difficult time with two of my princely supporters on just those grounds."

"We all know about Philip of Hesse," I said. Philip was the host of the great Marburg Colloquy between Luther and Zwingli and their colleagues in 1529 and a strong supporter of the Reformation in Luther's later years. His pleading to be allowed to have two wives at one time, like the biblical patriarchs did, was, with reluctance, agreed to by Luther and Melanchthon before the wedding in 1540. When news leaked out, it was very discrediting to the Reformation cause.[8]

I did not want to stir Luther up on another issue where his leadership has been generally faulted. But I was still curious. "Who was the other?"

"Frederick the Wise, of course," replied Luther. "Even now I hate to criticize him because we could have accomplished nothing without his support. He was wise about ruling, but not too wise in his private life. He never married, but had a mistress and a couple of children by her. That's why the Electorship went to his brother John after his death."[9]

"So we should not be surprised by it, this recurrent weakness of the flesh?" I asked.

"That is a part of it," Luther answered sadly. "I now know more than I once did about how vulnerable public leaders are to this temptation. I'd heard some pretty gripping tales in eternity. But this is nothing new. Read the Italian poet Dante; I suppose you know about him. I don't have much use for purgatory, but he shows all the varieties of love gone wrong—especially among leaders.

"Still, we can't give up on the gift of marriage and the wonderful things God can accomplish in it. Sometimes better things happen in the next generation; it isn't always downhill. Frederick's brother John was a widower from an early age, but his son and Frederick's nephew John Frederick had a wonderful marriage to the lovely Princess Sybil. I still remember how kind they were to my family during my many illnesses."

I would have loved to ask Luther about his marriage and his family but I wanted to continue on the sexual front. "What about gays and lesbians in the church, Dr. Luther?" I blurted out, evidencing my own discomfort about asking a most pressing question for our time.

Luther, who had been headed for the door, sat down—something I had never seen him do before. He sunk rather deeply into the chair and rubbed his chin, as if thinking about what to say.

"All right, since you've asked, I'll tell you. And

what I'll tell you first is what I told you before. I just don't know. You'll have to work that out as the church in your time. From what I hear, that won't be easy. I must admit that this was another issue like the ordination of women that just floored me when I first heard it discussed in heaven. I can't say that I understand, or can understand as a man of my time, all that is involved."

Since he seemed to be in no hurry now, I decided to pursue the question further. "You've said on other issues that you would not tell us what to do. That's fair enough on this issue as well. But then you have on other issues gone ahead and at last made some comments. Will you do that in this case as well?"

He paused. "You may think that when I say I don't understand, I'm just avoiding the question. That's not true. We know something about the matters that you mention from the Bible, of course, and that has authority when rightly interpreted. I know something about these matters from my own time; you could not live for decades in monastic life and not be aware of the various places that people found relief from a vow of chastity that they could not carry out. But even these words—gay and lesbian—belong to your time and only partly translate for me.

"But there are some things I can say. I've mentioned the Bible, and I don't think you can run past that. You struggled through to a credible answer—

though not the only possible answer—on the ordination of women. You need to do that here too.

"Yet the Bible alone cannot settle this. There is a sad human tendency to underestimate what we might have called 'the strength of the flesh' or what you call 'the power of sexuality.'" He said the last word very slowly, in five syllables, as if he were trying to ponder what it might mean.

"Very good. Don't underestimate. It's the same matter we were discussing with our princes and your presidents. The impulse to love, to bodily love, is strong and will not be denied, except for the rare few who really have the gift of celibacy.

"I've heard in heaven of a Dr. Sigmund Freud who has some views about this. Apparently he's very controversial. But he shows that it doesn't take Christian faith to understand the strength of this drive. In fact, I sometimes think some kinds of faith may cloud the vision, making people naive about life. So don't give in to the flesh, but don't underestimate it either. It's a hard task to discern God's will in these matters. But God will help you."

My mind was reeling. I wanted to ask about so many different things. Was sexuality an order of creation, a social construction, or both? Were Christians less wise in their generation than the children of this world? What should be done with or about gays and lesbians in the church? But now Luther was getting ready to leave. "Any other urgent questions, Lull?" he asked with a smile.

"I know we'll be talking about war and peace. That really divides Christians today," I continued.

"Lull, it's too late to go into that topic. The question of war divided Christians in my day as well, and the issue was one I was called to address again and again. I always felt Augustine was on the right track with his 'just war' concept, but that very few wars really qualified as just. Frederick the Wise was very cautious about taking up arms, feeling that most princes were hotheads and all too ready for others to die for their momentary causes. He had a good restraining effect on me."

"Is there anything simple that I can say at the synods?" I asked.

"There's nothing simple about it. Still you must say something because, as I understand your government today, you are all the princes. You can't just let them handle these matters for you. So perhaps it's best to remind them what I always tried to teach—that a Christian may not take up arms for self-defense, but that a Christian must take up arms to defend a neighbor in need."

I had the feeling that this would make both the doves and the hawks in our church angry, or at least really confuse them. So I acknowledged that Luther was about to leave. "Thank you," I offered gratefully, "it has been a real privilege."

"It's been a pleasure for me, Lull," he said. "Maybe I'll see you someday in Germany. I understand you are coming back. I was quite busy the last time you were there, but who can say about the next time? And do be careful with your books."

I was thrilled to think that this might not be the end, because there was so much more to discuss. But I did want this visit to end on a different note. So I asked Luther whether he would once again read one of my favorite passages from his writings.

"You know I hate hearing my thoughts in English," he said, "but I will read a piece that I hope isn't too long. That may be a challenge, given my writing."

"Try this," I suggested, handing him my Luther volume open to a place near the conclusion of his "Meditation on Christ's Passion" (1519).

"Yes," said Luther, "I'll read this with pleasure. I'd rather be remembered for this than for some of my words, which have brought only trouble."

The treatise in question is one in which Luther addresses the right way to receive the full benefit from the passion and death of Christ. He is quite firm that you must learn to see a personal, sinful separation from God in the human rejection of Jesus. But he also warns you not to get stuck on your knees, but to see the even deeper lesson of the Christ as God's love for you. And so Luther read:

> You must no longer contemplate the suffering of Christ (for this has already done its work and terrified you), but pass beyond that and see his friendly heart and how this

heart beats with such love for you that it
impels him to bear with pain your conscience and your sin. Then your heart will
be filled with love for him, and the confidence of your faith will be strengthened.

Luther paused. "Is that enough?" I shook my head
no, and he continued:

Now continue to rise beyond Christ's heart
to God's heart and you will see that Christ
would not have shown this love for you if
God in his eternal love had not wanted this,
for Christ's love for you is due to his obedience to God. Thus you will find the divine
and kind paternal heart, and, as Christ says,
you will be drawn to the Father through
him. Then you will understand the words
of Christ, "For God so loved the world that
he gave his only son . . ." (John 3:16). We
know God aright when we grasp him not in
his might or wisdom (for then he proves
terrifying), but in his kindness and love.[10]

"You've chosen well, Lull," said Dr. Luther. But
if you are going to speak to those Lutherans who
like to use my name, don't give the impression our
talk of bishops and princes is what I would most
want to say to them. Stress the 'kind paternal
heart of God' and you will be speaking for me."

The Third Visit
Eisenach, Germany, July 1998

If my first visit from Luther was the result of editing his writings, and the second came about when I was almost killed by his books, the third visit seemed occasioned by a far more humble fact. One night in Eisenach, after a day of visiting Luther sites, including climbing all over the Wartburg Castle, I had a huge dinner and ate so many dumplings that I was feeling uncomfortable at bedtime. So even though it might have been a little risky in the middle of what had not long ago been East Germany, I decided that I had no choice but to go out for a late-night walk.

We were staying in the Hotel Thuringer Hof in the Karlsplatz. The manager asked if he could help me as I headed out the door at 11 P.M. I told him that I needed a little walk and thought I might go out for a beer. "We have a fine bar in this establishment," he told me, in perfect British English, "but if you need a walk, by all means try the Schwarze Katze in Lutherstrasse."

The Black Cat Tavern in Luther Street! Now that appealed to me. So I headed out. On a hill in the distance I could see by the bright moonlight the Wartburg Castle itself. Here was the very town where Luther had been a schoolboy, and where years later he had returned to live for ten months in hiding at the castle, growing a beard and disguising himself as Knight George. Here was the historic town of the Bach family, and the church where the great musician was baptized. Even though I am an outgoing fellow, I was enjoying my solitary late-night walk through the almost empty streets of the town center of Eisenach, seeing again by silence and in moonlight the places we had visited during the day.

Of course, you will not be surprised to hear that I never made it to the Schwarze Katze—or at least not directly. After what Luther had said to me only a few months ago, when he visited my rebuilt office, I had thought that I might run into him in Germany. Was it really the excess of dumplings that sent me out on that walk, or was it a premonition that here in this historic town I might encounter Dr. Luther yet one more time?

I had almost reached the marketplace when I realized that Luther was walking beside me. "Hello, Lull," he said cheerfully. "Welcome to Germany. I think I am right in saying 'Welcome back.'"

"Dr. Luther," I replied, "this is a pleasure. And so soon after our last visit. You said that I might see you in Germany," I added.

"And so you do," he answered.

"To tell you the truth, I thought that I might see you at the Wartburg Castle earlier today," I continued, but Luther looked horrified at the idea. Even in the moonlight and with some great cloak half covering his face, his distaste for the place was evident.

"Not likely," said Luther, "though I have learned in heaven to be a little more hesitant to say 'Never,'" he added quickly. "That is one place that I'll keep my distance from if at all possible—even to this day."

"Surely nothing could harm you there now," I said.

"True enough," said Luther. "And, by the way, you can stop looking around so anxiously as we walk. You won't have any trouble from the locals tonight as long as you are walking with me."

"Thank you, sir," I answered, relieved that he had sensed my discomfort in being out for a night stroll in a strange city. For the next hour or two—however long it lasted—we walked all around that city, never passing anyone directly, but often seeing people in the distance—a couple walking home or a truck making some night delivery. "Do these visits always take place by night?"

"Mine do, mostly," replied Luther, "yet 'always' is another of those words to be avoided in the kinds of encounters we are now discussing. I think it's tradition mostly. I don't know why it could not happen in the daylight. We've talked before of the ghost of Hamlet's father. Marley's ghost haunted Scrooge about this hour on Christmas Eve. And the devil visited Dr. Faust for the first time in his study at night, but that was quite different, of course. Those were all just stories."[1]

"Well, Dr. Luther," I continued, trying to turn the conversation from ghosts to Luther himself, "I wanted to ask you about the Wartburg, but perhaps I should not bring it up, as it is a source of distress to you."

"I don't mind talking about it," replied Luther, perhaps a little sharply. "I just don't want to get too close. The memories—and they are mostly unhappy ones—are still quite intense. I'm told these fade after a long season, but I haven't been dead quite 500 years yet, so these things seem like yesterday. But what was it that you wanted to ask?"

"I believe you were a schoolboy here in Eisenach, Dr. Luther," I began, suddenly formulating a whole line of questioning that would clear up some questions about Luther's life story. Of course, I had learned that these visits often came to an end rather abruptly, so I did not know how far I might get or whether Luther had come to see me with something more specific in mind than a welcome to an American tourist.

"Yes," answered Luther, in quite a jolly way, "yes, indeed. I was a schoolboy here at the School of Saint George—the patron saint of this town. I started school here exactly five hundred years ago as you count time, and I fell in love with the town at once. I've loved it ever since. Town, Ja; Castle, Nein."[2]

"Which is just what I wanted to ask, sir," I continued. "Were you aware of the Wartburg Castle when you were a schoolboy here?"

"Aware of it!" replied Luther. "How could you miss it? It would be like failing to notice the moon tonight. They say you have sons, so you must know something about what children are like. We frightened each other with ghost stories about it. We even wondered whether there might be a spare dragon left up there that Saint George had not gotten around to killing. We had no idea of the saint's time or country. We thought he was a local knight. That's why I took the name Knight George when I was living in the castle in disguise years later."

"Was the Wartburg Castle the most wonderful building you had ever seen up to that point?" I asked.

He laughed. "I suppose you think there wasn't much in Eisleben, my birthplace, and you are right about that. Nor were there tourists in those days coming to see the house where Luther was born, and the house where Luther died, and to buy postcards, and beer mugs, and tea sets, and jewelry, and maps, and all those things that you all take home to all your friends.[3] Buying gifts was bad enough in my day; I could never find anything for the children when I was traveling. I always had to ask Katie to get something in Wittenberg and slip it to me when I returned so that I could pretend that I had brought it for the children. I was more confident before the emperor at Worms than trying to decide what to buy in the gift stalls of Nuremberg."

The theologian seemed in a wonderful and expansive mood, and as always during these conversations, I had no sense of the speed or slowness of the passing of time, if any time passed at all. We did walk, and I knew that the next morning because I had the kind of extra slight ache in my limbs that you have when you go much farther on foot in a day than you are accustomed.

But Luther continued. "When I was very young, too young to remember, my family moved to Mansfeld. There were finer buildings there, such as the castle of the Counts. But the first really wonderful building that I ever saw was the great cathedral or Dom in Magdeburg when I went off there to school when I was thirteen years old. Have you been there?" he asked hopefully.

"Yes," I reported, "we went there last week, just after Berlin. It is a wonderful building, although so much of the rest of the city is so depressingly modern. I understand it was largely destroyed in the Second World War."

"You've had a rather bloody century yourself, Lull, haven't you?" asked Luther. I nodded, having learned that there was little point in trying to answer such questions, especially when he was quite right. Luther continued, "I know how you look down on my century for the Peasants' War and especially on those who came after us for what you call the Thirty Years' War—supposedly fought in the name of religion. But your century can match, and even surpass, mine for bloodshed.

"In any case, let's stick to the topic. If you were impressed by that great church in Magdeburg, imagine what it meant to me as a thirteen-year-old boy from a tiny town. And it was still being finished when I was there for my first year of study. I loved that church, and all the great churches of Magdeburg. I was proud to know that we had something that wonderful in Germany."

"Perhaps that's why you don't seem to have been all that impressed with Rome and its churches when you were sent there on business by your order," I suggested.

"You mean I left my heart in Magdeburg? Perhaps I did. To tell you the truth, I was so intensely caught up in my work and the conflicts within my order I hardly noticed Italy when I made that trip. I've been told I missed a lot."[4]

"Did you ever go back to Magdeburg?" I asked.

"Yes," replied Luther. "I know I was there several times in 1524 to settle disputes, to preach, and to celebrate the acceptance of the Reformation in this great city. It was then I was able to see that the cathedral had been completed by my old enemy Albrecht of Mainz, who was (contrary to church custom) the archbishop of both Magdeburg and Mainz at the same time. Of course, he was not around anymore when I came there to preach the gospel."

"And then you came here to Eisenach the next year?" I asked.

"Yes," Luther continued, "when I was fourteen my father decided he wanted a different school, a better school, so he sent me to Saint George's. I studied Latin there to prepare for the university at Erfurt. There was some hope that I could stay with relatives, but that didn't work out. It was a struggle for my parents to pay for this schooling, but I hardly gave that a thought at the time. I suppose children seldom do. I liked my studies for the most part; I also remember the singing—and there were many opportunities for that."

"There's a debate about which house you actually lived in," I began, but Luther cut me off.

"Don't start out on that," he said sharply. "We'll stir up a bigger hornet's nest than the Reformation if we get into quarrels like that. I do chuckle at all the signs that say, 'Luther slept here' and other things along those lines. How would I remember which house after all the changes through the centuries? That's not what sticks in one's mind."

"They also say," I offered, trying another line, "that there were good and pious people here, lay-persons deeply interested in religion."

"That is true," said Luther, "and that is something I still remember. They were the kind of folks that I thought about so often when we feared that the Reformation might fail. They had such hopes for new life in the church. I think I could easily have become someone like them—perhaps a lawyer attached to a princely court in a small town like this. I like to think that I would have been part of the lay movement that supported the Reformation so strongly. I might have gone to hear the great Reformer preach—whoever it might have been—when he came through town."

"Would the Reformation have taken place without you?" I asked, and Luther was visibly irritated.

"Look, Lull," he continued. "I have had my blind spots. But I always knew that if the gospel was being restored, this was the work of the Holy Spirit and not the work of Luther. It was an honor, and at times a great burden, almost too great to bear, to play a part—perhaps a large part—in it. But I never imagined that it was my doing."

"But you didn't become a lawyer," I remarked, hoping he would continue this narrative of his life. "You entered the monastery and became a monk, to the great displeasure of your family, especially your father."

"What I see clearly now," said Luther, "is how my decision really crushed the hopes they had for me and, I suppose, for themselves as well, to be the parents of a successful son. The decision always seemed sudden to them, but you can imagine—you who work with students training to be pastors today—that such decisions are rarely made on impulse, however bad the thunderstorm. I had thought about the religious life for a long time, perhaps all the way back to my Magdeburg and Eisenach days.

"There were, as you were saying, wonderful devout laypersons in places like this, with their studying, and their praying, and their gathering, and their works of mercy, which gave great credibility to Christianity. But the signal always came through from the church itself that if you were really serious about the faith you would go ever farther and enter religious life as a priest or a monk or—if you were a girl—as a nun."

"And yet you did not find happiness with the Augustinians,"[5] I suggested.

"Is that right?" asked Luther, seeming to speak more to himself than to me. "Do we ever know when we are happy in the middle of things? I complained a lot as a schoolboy here in Eisenach, and yet what a lifelong love of reading, and especially of the Latin authors, I got here—especially Cicero.[6] I complained a lot in the monastery. I did drive poor Staupitz almost crazy with my struggles in Erfurt. Do you know that he sent me off to Wittenberg to lecture for one year in 1508—on Aristotle!"

"What were your first impressions of Wittenberg?" I asked.

"Pretty disappointing, to tell you the truth, Lull," he answered. "It was a little place—nothing like Magdeburg or Erfurt or even Eisenach. It was not nearly the town that it came to be when the university grew and started to draw students from all of Europe. I suppose it had only a couple of thousand people, and the university had perhaps a couple hundred students. In those days it was a center for brewing beer, and not very good beer either.

"I do remember vividly from that year that Frederick's great project of building the castle church was just being completed. Master Lucas Cranach, the painter, was decorating the insides, and Frederick's huge collection of relics was being installed. I was never very enthusiastic about them, even before I became a critic of the church. But I was scrambling all that year as a young lecturer, one step ahead of the students, trying to emulate the best of my own teachers in my approach.

"I don't know what all Staupitz had in mind. Perhaps he saw it as a kind of trial year for my eventual appointment there a couple of years later. But I half think he did it to get rid of me for a while, to 'have a break,' as you Americans would say. And he sent me to Rome a couple of years later, perhaps for the same reason."

"And then you went back to Wittenberg to stay. When, in 1511?" I asked.

"That's right," replied Luther. "The first year I finished my doctorate in theology, for which Frederick the Wise agreed to pay, so that I could become professor of the Bible—which happened the next year. Say, are we doing a review of my life? Well, I don't mind. It is quite pleasant to stroll around these old and new streets with you. Are you feeling a little more assured about your safety?"

"Yes, Dr. Luther," I replied.

"Well, fire away, Lull," he said laughing, "Now we've gotten to Wittenberg with quite a short stop in Erfurt. That's fine. And what questions do you have about those years?"

"Many," I answered, so that if our time was headed to an end soon, I might receive a warning to come quickly to whatever was most important still on my list. "But what scholars would like to know is when your 'Reformation experience' took place. Did you come to your distinctive understanding of the gospel early in the time in Wittenberg, or as late is 1518, as some now suggest?"

"Oh, Lull," he replied, "how I wish I knew! Then we could put them out of their misery. You could write the definitive article, refuting once and for all any other opinions. What fun that would be.

"But seriously, you must understand that these matters are far less clear to me. 'Reformation breakthrough'? There were moments of insight as early as in the Erfurt years, and times of deep confusion well into the Wittenberg years, even after the indulgence controversy began. These autobiographical searches for inner turning points are impossible. We live forward, but understand backward, and those are quite different things."

I was considering all this, but Luther turned the problem back on me.

"Let me show you what I mean by questioning you for a little while. You are thought to be a Luther scholar, I assume."

I looked uncertain. "Well, at least a proficient teacher of Luther?" he continued.

I nodded—hesitant to claim too much but wondering above all where he was headed.

"When did you get that status? I don't think that was your doctoral training. Wasn't that in systematic something—systematic theology, perhaps, a very odd term if you won't take offense?"

"No, sir," I agreed. "No offense taken. You'll have to get acquainted with Karl Barth one of these days in heaven. You could have quite a conversation about 'systematic theology.' He didn't much like it either."

"I know a little about Barth, Lull," he said, "but I am still mostly busy with my friends—and enemies—in my own century. I think I was telling you about Henry VIII and Leo X last time and our Bible study group. I didn't tell you that we tried to have Carlstadt in there too, but it was just too difficult even for heaven.[7]

"I am eager to get to know some people who lived after my time, but they may not be the same ones that you would seek out, Lull. I am just getting to know this Martin Chemnitz a little better.[8] I think you know what quarrels there were among my followers after my death. They called him the second Martin because his peacemaking efforts really saved the Lutheran church from internal collapse. I'm coming to understand how much the preservation of the gospel owes to his work. So I may be a long time getting around to the twentieth century—except for some visits like this.

"Now, I will admit that I did make a special effort to get to know Johann Sebastian Bach, who comes to mind here in Eisenach and in so many other places that I like to revisit. There are almost as many 'Bach slept here' signs as 'Luther slept here.' Long ago I made special arrangements to meet him and thank him for his music. We are more up to date on music in heaven than we are on theology. I hope that doesn't disappoint you."

"No, sir," I replied. "I think I understand that very well. But somehow we've gotten off the point—your point, Dr. Luther. I think it was the mention of 'systematic theology.'"

"Quite right," said Luther, taking things back under his control. "Well, you can't tell me when you had your 'Luther breakthrough.' Was it as a student, and if so, at what level of study? Or was it when you were a pastor? Or a later when you were a professor? Which year, and in which course? Or was it in your writing? With which project? You see how hopeless it is. You can't tell me when you had your 'Luther breakthrough' and I can't tell you, after 500 years, when I had my 'Reformation breakthrough.'"

"And yet," I ventured, "there were decisive moments along the way once the controversy about indulgences boiled over."

"Now, that is easier to settle," said Luther. "Public events are much more reliable markers than shifts in thinking. There were two key moments between the start of the trouble in 1517 and the Diet of Worms in 1521. The first was my presentation at Heidelberg in the spring of 1518. It was the annual meeting of the monks of the Augustinian order. And as 'punishment' for all the trouble that I had stirred up, I was asked to make a major presentation. At first I thought this would be fun, for I've always liked having an audience—as you have, Lull—but I was told to keep it positive and by all means not to mention the pope. My order had invested a lot in me, and they didn't want me to fail.

"So I struggled all through Lent in the spring of 1518. It is easier to criticize than to construct. I found part of what I wanted to say in the sermons I preached in that season. You know, of course, that what I finally presented was my understanding of the theology of the cross, and how its proclamation of the God who is hidden and surprising contrasts with the theology of glory, which is usually what the churches like and what people would do if they were God. That was a breakthrough, although only a few of my younger colleagues saw it at the time. But after this I never again read the Bible in the same way."

"And the other moment?" I asked.

"Can you guess?" he asked with a smile. "You are the one who teaches Luther, not me."

"Was it the debate with Eck in Leipzig?" I carefully asked.

"Of course," said Luther, "good for you, although that was hardly a stumper. That was in June of 1519—about fifteen months after Heidelberg. Up until that time I didn't realize how fundamental, how sweeping, was my criticism of the church and its structure. After Eck called me a Hussite, I looked into the matter and discovered—first to my horror, and then to increasing delight—that I shared all of Hus's critique of the church and more.[9] From then on I began to doubt that reform could be accepted by the whole church. Some friends, especially Melanchthon, were still hopeful in 1540, but my hope faded the last time in 1530 when the Augsburg Confession, so carefully constructed to please the Romans, was not accepted."[10]

"By 1519 Melanchthon had come to Wittenberg to teach?" I asked.

"Yes," said Luther, "and it meant that he was with me for almost the whole story, except the very beginning. He was so young when he first arrived that we all made jokes about how a mere boy was going to be much help to us. But when he first stood up to speak and gave his inaugural lecture, the jokes stopped. Within a few weeks we were firm friends and stayed constant coworkers ever after.

"Are you going to Wittenberg on this trip? I hope you haven't already been there. It would be really grand to have one of our visits there."

"We'll be there in about a week," I reported.

"Well," said Luther, "it's possible. We will have to see. These things are more complicated than I can take time to explain just now. And you've had your share of my time, if you don't mind my saying so. Not that I don't enjoy these visits and your questions. So what else tonight? Where were we?"

"You were speaking of Eck, Dr. Luther, and that he actually helped you to see how deep your questions about the church were."

"You'll be asking next whether we've been in heavenly Bible study together," chuckled Luther. "No, not yet. I suppose in eternity Eck and I will have to get together sooner or later. You see, Lull, it is easier to be reconciled with more distant opponents like the King of England or the Medici Pope than with people that you knew face to face. Eck and I started out as friendly acquaintances. Then we exchanged a few blows in print. But Eck really worked me over at Leipzig. I think he understood better than I did myself at the time how radical my views were. To be fair, he was one of those who loved the old church and who thought that firm papal authority was the only way to stave off chaos. Once Eck and I diverged, he was always active against me, pleading with Frederick the Wise, stirring up trouble with Frederick's cousin Duke George in Leipzig, and even making trips to Rome to stir the pot against me there."

"So you knew when you came home from Leipzig in the summer of 1519 that your critique of the church extended even to the level of doubting papal authority. But what followed first, instead of trouble, was an explosion of writing, so many of your books that are best known and most highly regarded."

"Perhaps you've had a time like this in your own life, Lull," he suggested, "when the very intensity of events for a time acts as a stimulus to work. The moves to crush me took a little time, and the church was very eager not to offend my prince. For my part, I didn't imagine that I could survive long, having set down the path that I had taken. I had a lot that I wanted to say, about the sacraments especially, but also about faith and good works, about how Reformation might take place in Germany, despite the opposition of the bishops, if the princes would take the lead. Then too I wanted to write a celebration of Christian freedom in honor of all the help I'd received from that theme in Saint Paul, especially his letter to the Galatians.

"All of that got finished in a year and a half, at the same time that I was preaching and spending part of my time defending myself and fighting off attempts to send me to Rome. It was a lot of writing, but then I always liked to work. And I kept up the pace rather well, I think, except later in the last ten years of my life, when I was often ill for months on end."[11]

A black cat crossed our path. Instead of feelings of dread, I thought with pleasure of the intensity of Luther's remembering and the privilege of hearing him on these great events. The cat also reminded me that I had been headed to the tavern, although that now seemed beside the point.

But Luther seemed to be thinking along the same lines. "Wouldn't it be great to sit and have a beer together?" he asked. I wondered how this would be possible, but he continued, "Of course I couldn't drink it, but I could sit with you. It's a warm summer night. Look at that tavern just ahead—we must be on what they now call Lutherstrasse. There are tables outside, so we don't need to disturb them inside—as my appearance would. You see, I'm under orders myself on excursions like this and I can't exceed my instructions and get all involved with my countrymen and all their problems with the new Germany. But you could go in and get two beers and we could sit out here facing the marketplace and finish our talk. I'd like to get as far as the Wartburg part of the story tonight."

It happened just as Luther suggested. I went in, bought two beers in the sleepy, smoky bar, where no one showed the least bit of curiosity about my presence. I took them out to the farthest table where he had settled down on a bench. "Where were we?" Luther asked, as I began to sip my beer. He held his, and I thought once he sniffed it, but I could have been wrong. He certainly did not drink it.

"I suppose we were up to 1520," I said. "You were writing so many of your major works. But you were working as if you were a man condemned."

"There was no 'as if' about it," retorted Luther. "I was a man condemned. By the middle of the summer of 1520, Leo X had issued the warning bull, which was delivered to me in Wittenberg in October.[12] In December, I burned that document and a lot of other books as well. Then, in January the pope excommunicated me. By April of 1521 I had to appear before Charles V at Worms and was condemned by him as well. It amazes me even now how fast it all happened, and yet how I was able to do so much theological work in the meantime. You can see why I was exhausted by the time I arrived at the Wartburg—physically and emotionally as well."

"Do you have any regrets about this part of your story?" I asked.

Luther looked puzzled for a moment, as if any part of it could possibly have been different—on his part or on the part of any of the other actors in the drama. But then he said, "I do regret burning the bull, and especially the books. A lot of evil has come from that. Too many books have been burned. I don't regret polemic and sharp debate, even though I know, Lull, that you think I went too far in many instances. And perhaps I did. But I can more easily defend a battle of words and ideas after all these centuries than I can the kind of mob action of the book burning.

"It was fun, I won't deny it—wonderful, wicked fun. But I soon learned how many others could play that game, and what disorder and hatred arose when people tried to settle matters by destroying." He mentioned that he admired a story he had heard recently that tells how, once book burning starts, there is no place to stop. He said he couldn't remember the name of the story or who had written it.[13] I was getting the impression that much time in heaven is spent in reading and on music—at least by Luther and his circle.

"And at Worms itself," I asked, "what was that like for you? They say you were received as a hero all through Germany as you made your way there, but once inside the city you were very frightened."

"Both are true," said Luther. "I was able to preach in a number of places on my way to the Diet;[14] through preaching I wanted to share my sense that the battle was not basically about Luther, but about what the message and life of the church would be. Some minor church official here in Eisenach made a public avowal, before a notary, that he had tried to stop me from preaching at Saint George's so that he could defend himself if there was trouble later. I tried to plant deep seeds of gospel in those years, hoping something would survive whatever happened to me.

"But when I came into the presence of the Imperial Court, I felt alone, even though many friends were with me. And there was great pressure on me to 'behave' when I came before the emperor. I think Charles was shocked when he finally saw me, shocked that it would come to this: that a ruler of his authority (for he was the most powerful man in the world at that time) actually had to be in the presence of, had to listen to—let alone argue with—a miner's son like me."[15]

"Yes," I said, "but you were also Dr. Luther, Professor Luther, by that time."

"Those were not necessarily honors in that family and at that court," answered Luther, almost bitterly. "And of course I was torn about Frederick, my own prince. He had always played things so carefully, never even having direct contact with me. Everything had to be handled through Spalatin and others of his court. We always had to be more cautious than I wanted to be. And yet he was my good prince, and I did not want to make life impossible for him. He himself had embarked on a risky course when he chose to protect me. I wished sometimes I could just disappear and make things easier for him."

"In the end it seems that he did what he could for you, got you into and out of Worms safely," I ventured and Luther nodded. "At least the safe-conduct held."

"I think," Luther said, "there was such a shock even 100 years later about what had happened to Hus; he set out for the Council of Constance with a safe-conduct and was seized and executed anyway. Of course, that was the fault of the Dominicans. But still, the people remembered, and the court did not want to create another martyr by doing something rash. But there was always the risk some would take things into their own hands. I was happy to learn much later that Frederick had been quite pleased with my conduct at the Diet. He told Spalatin I had done very well, holding forth in German and in Latin, before the emperor and all the nobles."[16]

The buildings of the town blocked the view of the castle from where we were sitting, but I knew that Luther's thoughts had turned in that direction. I ventured this: "And then you did disappear. On the way home from Worms you were kidnapped, or so it seemed, and you dropped out of sight."

"Yes," said Luther, "although people had their suspicions. But it did buy some precious time for Charles to get distracted by events elsewhere while I was hidden in the Wartburg."

I continued, "So may I ask, Dr. Luther, over these beers that we are sharing, what was so bad about your ten months there?"

"I'll try to explain it, Lull," he said, "but it may be difficult to feel the intensity with which so many different factors came together. I've mentioned exhaustion. I had health problems that you wouldn't want to hear about.[17] Then there was sheer fear for my life. I had a narrow escape in Worms and no promise that the emperor would not send some troops to find me.

"After a time there was terrible news from Wittenberg, troubles and disturbances of all sorts. Once I made a secret visit back there, in my knight's disguise and great beard. I slipped into town and back out again without being recognized by anyone who could make trouble. I thought things were all right, but they weren't. So I returned a second time—this time to stay after things really got out of hand after Christmas of 1521. People were rioting, priests were marrying, strange prophets appeared claiming that they brought direct revelations from God. It all made me uneasy for the town and its people.

"You know what Paul says in 2 Corinthians 11 about having so many problems, and yet hardest of all the hardship is anxiety for the churches. I daresay you have days like that for your school, especially when trees come crashing into your office."

"You haven't mentioned the devil," I said. "I thought that he might have been especially present at the Wartburg, and that's why you still avoid it."

"So you saw the place where I am said to have thrown an ink bottle at the devil? I don't remember. I probably threw more than one. But the great comfort of heaven for me, Lull," said Luther, "is that the case is closed on that Evil One. He cannot harm me or lure me now. But generally it is hopeless to talk to people from your time about these matters, because you are so proud of 'how far you've come.' No, I keep my distance from the Wartburg Castle because many of my days there were among the most unhappy of my life."

"And yet people treated you kindly," I added, and Luther nodded vigorously. "You did good work there, some of your best. You wrote remarkable things including the commentary on Mary's Song, the Magnificat, and the *Treatise against Monastic Vows*. And of course you translated the New Testament into German. So perhaps good did come out of evil and, perhaps, strength did come out of weakness."

"You are preaching to me, Lull, which I don't resent, and you are even doing it rather well," said Luther, getting up from his bench, "but it's too late for any more tonight. I've promised to do my best to see you one last time, in my own Wittenberg. I had my happiest days there, of course, but some sad ones too, as I hope we'll be able to discuss." We were now walking back toward my hotel.

"Can you tell me when to expect you?" I asked, hoping I wasn't stepping across some heavenly boundary. Luther waved his hand in impatience. "All right," I continued, "it will be a pleasure if and when it happens, but thanks so much for the walk tonight."

"Thank you for the beer," said Luther, "but aren't we forgetting something? I always read a little at the end of these visits. Well, I guess we can't do that tonight, as you don't seem to be carrying around that enormous volume of my writings. Too bad, as I've come to enjoy that ritual."

I smiled and reached into my pocket, pulling out a folded copy of some photocopied pages. "Whenever I travel to your places, Dr. Luther, I carry something you wrote with me. I was reading today some of the letters that you wrote from the Wartburg to your friends in Wittenberg. Try this letter to Master Philipp."

"Let's see," said Luther. "Yes, this is just right. It would be a good conclusion to our talk. It's turning cold, so perhaps I'll read just a few lines." And he read this:

> I definitely do not want you to worry about me in any way. As far as I am concerned, all is well, except that the troubles of my soul have not yet ceased, and the former weakness of the spirit and faith persists. My life in seclusion means nothing. Since I never was engaged in the exposition of the Word by my own volition, I am now excluded from it with great peace of heart. That is the state of affairs as far as I personally am concerned. However, for the glory of the Word and for the strengthening of others and in turn for my own strengthening, I would rather burn among glowing coals than rot here alone half alive—may God grant, not dead. But who knows whether Christ does not wish to accomplish more by this plan, not only in my case but also in all others. We spoke so many times of faith and hope for the things not seen. Come on, let's test at least once a small part of Christ's teaching, since things have come to pass this way at the call of God and not through our doing. Even though I should perish, the gospel will not lose anything. [18]

I was enjoying this, Luther himself rebuking Luther's Wartburg fears, which still lingered after 500 years. I also was thinking that it was cold, and that I would not have called this long excerpt "a few lines." Then suddenly I was back at the door of the Thuringer Hof Hotel, and Luther was gone.

As I entered the lobby, I was astonished to see that it was only 11:15 P.M. "Not much of a walk, sir," said the manager as I waited at the elevator. "But good night, sir." And then to someone else behind the desk he said, in German that I could perfectly well understand, "That American went for a walk but apparently couldn't even follow my simple directions and find his way to the Black Cat Tavern."

The Fourth Visit
Wittenberg, Germany, July 1998

A few days later we were in Wittenberg, and I was doubly excited—that I was seeing Wittenberg and that I hoped to see Luther again. He had told me during our midnight walk in Eisenach that he would try to see me one last time in his old town.

As for Wittenberg, I had been there only once before. It had been two years earlier, spending a very frustrating half day with a guided tour in which we weren't even able to see the town church (not on their list of appropriate sights)—which was the one place I was most eager to see in the whole town. Fortunately, two friends and I slipped into the church in the evening for an organ concert (Italian organ music in Luther's church, which is either a great irony or a great breakthrough), and the friendly staff allowed us to spend a few minutes after the concert poking around and examining the great altar painting that commemorates Luther—a cooperative effort by the Lucas Cranachs, Senior and Junior.

The great central panel of the painting depicts Christ and the disciples at the Lord's Supper at a round table, with the various reformers as the disciples. Luther is at first hard to find, because he is portrayed with the beard that he grew when he was Knight George hiding in the Wartburg. To the left is a picture of Melanchthon baptizing, with help from the artist Lucas Cranach, something of a surprise as Melanchthon was a layperson and is unlikely ever to have done this. On the right is John Bugenhagen hearing confession, a reminder of something that often surprises modern folks— that the Lutheran Reformation intended to retain private confession and absolution, at least as an option.[1]

Beneath the Lord's Supper is a rectangular panel that shows the Wittenberg congregation on the left, the crucified Christ in the center, and, on the right, Luther in the pulpit of the town church preaching to them. It is a characteristic pose, but it strikes the viewer as both funny and sad that Luther is so far away from the congregation. If you know about his disappointment at the end of his life, you will sense that this arrangement of the parts of the painting is probably not an accident. A good friend like Lucas Cranach would have understood very well and arranged the picture appropriately.

It was a very hot July afternoon in Wittenberg. I was again in the town church admiring the great painting when Luther himself greeted me. "Lull," he exclaimed, "so good to see you! And here you are in one of my favorite places. So much has changed in this town, but I can still come back to this church with unmixed pleasure and remember the best Wittenberg days.

"But it's too hot to stay inside. Let's go for a walk around the town and along the river. We will have more privacy. I am so excited that you are here. What do you think of what they now call Lutherstadt—Luther's Town?"

We walked toward the Castle Church. As we made our way, I began to tell him of my impressions. It had been thrilling to visit the Castle Church in this end of town, a part of what had once been the palace of Frederick the Wise. It was wonderful to see where the theses had been posted (if they were posted—Luther refused to settle this matter), to see the graves of Luther and Melanchthon, of Frederick the Wise and John the Steadfast. But something about the building left me cold. I tended to blame the Prussians, who had done substantial renovations near the end of the nineteenth century.

"The troubles go back much farther," said Luther, apparently happy to act as my tour guide. "The church was burned down in 1760 when it was hit by artillery fire during one of the many wars of that century. I will admit that the Prussians redecorated it in their grand style about 100 years ago. Have you seen what they did to me in the so-called cathedral in Berlin, where I have to stand as a statue with Zwingli and Calvin? Actually, Frederick is there too; I should ask him what he thinks of all this Prussian pomp."

It was always happening in these talks. We went along as if we were two friendly acquaintances having a nice visit, and then Luther would say something that would remind me of the unusual meeting of two worlds that our conversations made possible. He could just ask Frederick about such things? That would make historical scholarship a lot easier.

We now sat down on a bench just behind the Castle Church, out in a meadow, looking back at the backside of its mighty tower. I remembered that I wanted to ask many questions. "Could you tell me about coming back here in 1522, in the midst of the troubles? How did you manage to calm things down?"

"So we are going to continue my life story. That's always satisfying," chuckled Luther. "Perhaps you don't exactly see me as a calming influence. But I was, at least that time. It was the middle of Lent, in March of 1522. My return made quite a sensation, but I knew that I needed to move quickly and decisively. I preached every day for eight days, and the crowds held up well. People apparently were eager to hear me. It was partly because they were curious to see Dr. Luther again, but also because they were ready for another approach. They were weary of chaotic changes and the destruction in the churches.

"I preached in the parish church, telling the people how reformation should take place. I knew that if we could not restore order, Frederick would not put up with the situation, and that even if he did, the troubles here were likely to attract the unfavorable attention of the emperor. Charles V was not someone I was eager to see again anytime soon."[2]

"You promised that there would be changes," I added, "but how did you know what to do next? You didn't like the approach Carlstadt had taken."

"No," said Luther, "but I might never have gotten to the hard work of what to do about the Mass without being pushed into it by Carlstadt. At first I was feeling my way. It was very hard to know what to keep from the tradition, and what really needed to be changed. I wrote a couple of different orders of service—getting bolder and leaner as I went along. Of course, I knew from the beginning that worship had to point to the gospel rather than itself, just as my finger in that painting in the town church points to Christ crucified. And I knew that the Word had to be in the center of what we did when the people gathered."

"When my students read your writings on worship, they are surprised by how free you were, how willing to have local variations in the way that things were done," I added.

"Partly that was realism," said Luther. "I knew

that places like Nuremberg and Strasbourg looked to us for theological leadership, but I also knew, from my travels, that they valued their local traditions. So much of what shapes worship is the music, and that cannot be standardized. You have to work with local conditions, which are sometimes wonderful, and sometimes quite limited."

"You plunged in and wrote some hymns yourself," I said, and Luther smiled and nodded but seemed to have no comment on this. I suppose he finds our ways of singing his hymns quite different from those that were common in his time. "And, unlike some other reformers, you kept so much of what we now call 'the catholic tradition.'"

"Yes," said Luther, "I think you have a proverb about not throwing out the baby with the bathwater. I could never stand the destructive folks who wanted to tear down until nothing was left. We were able to build on so much of what went before, even if we had to purge things that had come in which led people to trust in themselves or even in the church rather than in Christ alone. But can you imagine trying to be Christians without Advent and Christmas, without Lent and Easter, as some do?"

We stood and began walking along the river, which was very pleasant in the heat of the July afternoon. Luther asked a few questions about our trip, about the adequacy of hotels and how we liked the food, and especially about the trains, which he seemed to find fascinating. Eventually he found another bench for us. As in all these conversations, though other people were around, they did not approach us but left us alone.

"It seems to me," I continued, "that it took you a long time to move beyond Wittenberg. When you finally got around to systematic visiting of the country churches, you were pretty shocked—enough to energize you to write those catechisms."

"For one thing," Luther replied, "we didn't have a free hand until after the death of Frederick. He was always cautious, right up until he received communion in both kinds on his deathbed from my friend Spalatin.[3] By then we were in the midst of the upheaval of the Peasants' War, and then soon after I was a very busy getting married."

"That would be 1525," I said. "I've always thought that was an amazing year for you, writing *The Bondage of the Will* against Erasmus, the troubles of the Peasants' War, the death of Frederick in the middle of it, and then your marriage in June. Was the decision to marry a sudden one?"

"In one way it was," replied Luther. "I had thought for some time, 'now if I were to marry, someone like Katie would be just right. She could handle me. But I probably don't have long to live, so it wouldn't be fair to her, or to any children that came.' But to my surprise, when I discussed the matter with my parents, they were very enthusiastic. They didn't mind at all that she had been a nun, which was an issue with some families."

"Did the death of Frederick give you a freer hand in this matter too?"

"Of course," replied Luther. "I knew that Frederick would be succeeded by his brother John, and that John would be Steadfast, as in the nickname he later came to have. He had long since made arrangements for his son John Frederick to be educated in the new ways of learning, and he was out in the open supporting what we were doing. I can't imagine what Frederick would have said or done about Luther with a wife."

"It is said that some of your circle didn't approve of your choice," I ventured as cautiously as I could, not naming Philipp Melanchthon and his wife Katherine.

"Good heavens, Lull!" exclaimed Luther. "That was a long time ago. Whatever any person may have thought at the time of the wedding, we all came to be very close. What grand celebrations we had for the holidays here. I had a wonderful circle of friends, as you know, and I could not have done my work without them."

"I'm not sure," I said, "that many who honor Dr. Luther think of your having fun. And yet I've heard that those evenings in Wittenberg—even many of the ordinary ones—were really quite delightful."

"Yes," said Luther, "in the evening we would eat and drink, play cards, and talk, and there was always someone interesting visiting. You have seen our house now—although sometimes when I come here I still think of it as the monastery. There were students and relatives and visitors from near and far, and of course—the children. Even royal visitors sometimes stayed with us."[4]

By now we were walking through the market-place, past the town church again, and down the street toward Melanchthon's house.

"You took to marriage rather well," I suggested, "at least from what I have read."

"Well, it was a surprise," said Luther. "Remember, I was over forty years old and rather set in my ways. You know, Lull, that men and women are quite different even when love is growing between them, as it did for me and my wife. It took time. They say that we left the monasteries and the convents for an easier life, but anyone who takes marriage and family life seriously would laugh at the idea that there is anything easy about it."

"Yet you had written as early as 1519 about what a great gift marriage is—something that was a fresh idea in contrast to much of the prevalent theology. And you wrote this not as one who knew it from the inside, for you were still a monk."[5]

"That's where my biblical work helped me," said Luther. "I came to see how much of the biblical world consists of people trying to serve and love God in the midst of everyday circumstances. Just look at the families in the book of Genesis. Abraham and Sarah have their problems, but their marrying and having children is clearly God-pleasing. And I learned from my ongoing contacts with my parents to think that I had been a fool to believe that my life in the monastery was of a 'higher order' than their life as a family."

"You saw them from time to time?" I asked.

"Yes," said Luther. "They had come to our wedding celebration, you know. My mother came back again to see Hans when he was born—a hard trip, but one well worth making, she said. My father died in 1530 when I was at the Coburg Castle awaiting news from Augsburg.

"That was a tense time, when the emperor was threatening us very strongly. Melanchthon had to go present our confession in Augsburg without me, since I was still under the ban. I was not allowed to come into the presence of Charles V. But I was also not able to attend my father's burial; it was simply not safe for me to travel in those months. My mother lived on until the next summer. You seem well informed about my family."

"We feel that we know your parents from the portraits that your friend Cranach painted," I said. "I understand he sketched them when they were in Wittenberg."

"Well, if you are going to be famous," said Luther smiling, "it helps to have an artist among your friends. You have other ways of doing it today."

I wasn't about to waste time discussing photography, if that was what Luther meant. Instead I asked about Cranach. "I sense you were good friends," I said, "and yet he painted not only portraits and biblical subjects, but seemed to specialize in nudes. I've always wondered what you thought about that."

"They were wonderful people, Lucas and Barbara," said Luther. "That's the first thing you have to understand. He had already been in Wittenberg for a long time when I arrived and was quite an accomplished painter. Frederick found him and hired him, just as he got Staupitz to go out and find me for the university. We used to say that we were like two animals in the Elector's zoo."

"But the nudes?" I asked, wondering where we might be headed.

"Yes, yes," said Luther, "we'll get there. Lucas was a painter, but he was a great man in so many other ways as well. He was a fine leader of the town, our mayor on several occasions. He was a printer. He knew theology too, or at least the Bible. I guess that of all of us involved in the Reformation, Lucas was the one who witnessed the whole story. As I said, he was already in Wittenberg in 1508 when I came for my trial year of teaching, and he was still living to go with John Frederick in exile to Weimar after that prince was released from prison. I had been long dead by that time, but God gave Lucas a good long life, and he continued painting until the last."

I didn't say anything. I wasn't going to ask again.

"All right," said Luther, "the nudes. The truth is that they did bother me at first, and very much. Cranach used to tease me about this, but there was nothing sordid about it. He helped me see that the body is not just the vessel of sin, as Luther the monk believed, but also somehow and at the same time still God's good creation."

"You met your wife at their house," I ventured, thinking we had gotten about as far as we were going to get with the nudes.

"Yes," said Luther, "and what a fortunate thing for me that she was assigned to live there. By that time the Cranach house was one of my major stops on my rounds in Wittenberg. So we had a natural way to get acquainted. I saw immediately how sharp she was—both sharp in the sense of intelligence, and sharp in the sense of pointed. I couldn't decide whether to be impressed or depressed. I had so little experience dealing with women."

"So you shared some of the joys of family life with the Cranachs," I said, "but some of the sorrows as well."

"You know, Lull, that joy and sorrow always come together," replied Luther, and he became thoughtful for a moment. "I was godfather to their daughter Anna and later Lucas was godfather to our son Hans. They were witnesses at our marriage. So there were joys.

"But we had our losses too. Our little daughter Elizabeth died after only a few months, and later we had the terrible loss of our wonderful Magdalena just when she was emerging as such a promising young woman. How the Cranachs and other friends wept with us then.[6]

"Yes, we bore each other's burdens. Once I had to minister to them because of the deep grief for the loss of their son Hans. He died while he was traveling in Italy—artists always seem to want to go there. They had not wanted him to make the trip, and they blamed themselves so harshly.

"We practiced what I used to call 'mutual consolation.'[7] There was never a season that we weren't burying someone or receiving some harsh news from friends or family at a distance."

"Who ministered to you, Dr. Luther?" I asked.

The reply came quickly. "Mostly it was Bugenhagen. He was a great pastor for the town and for the Luthers. I was not particularly suited for that work. You know that I became quickly impatient with people and what I considered their poor response to the gospel."

"Were you an impatient teacher?" I wondered.

Luther laughed. "Of course I was, at least most of the time. Master Philipp had so much patience that I sometimes wondered if he were dead. But then his exam questions were hopelessly difficult, and students did better to have me as judge of a disputation. None of us is completely consistent.

"I would sometimes find that a student won my sympathy, and I then could take great pains. I tended to have a special soft spot for anyone from the region of Eisleben and Mansfeld where I grew up. And Melanchthon could have a temper too. But generally we made a good team and balanced each other out well."

"We visited his house yesterday," I reported. The Melanchthon house has been wonderfully restored and tells the story of the Reformation from his point of view—which makes an interesting supplement and sometimes even a contrast to Luther. We were now standing in front of it.

"I'm jealous," said Luther, quickly adding, "not that you visited this house, of course, but of all the splendid equipment I understand that they have in there—words that are only names to me and most mysterious: 'computers, videos, earphones.'"

I was sure that in time these advantages would grace the Luther house as well. But I wanted to return our conversation to Luther's impatience with the town of Wittenberg and its reception of the Reformation. He was only too happy to talk about this.

"I see now that Wittenberg was not especially a bad place," admitted Luther, "and I see that I was an impatient person. But it is also true that people really are pretty lazy, Lull. I suppose that's why the whole system of indulgences and masses for the dead and relics and pilgrimage got started. People are pretty lazy, but also frightened. If there is a way they can address their fear of death and their deep sense of the loss of loved ones, they will do whatever is asked for the possible comfort.

"We wanted to take all that away, because we thought that it was both impossible and unnecessary to placate God. We wanted the gospel to shine forth in such a way that people would rejoice, lift their hearts, open their eyes, and spend their energy not on these needless religious good works, but on meeting the needs of their neighbors. They could do that not in order to please God, but because God had already come to them, in their sin and their weakness and their fear. At first the reception to such preaching was overwhelming. People greeted our fresh statement of the gospel with real joy.

"But then Christian freedom began to change. Paul saw it in Galatians: 'You were called to freedom, brothers and sisters; only do not use your freedom as an opportunity for self-indulgence, but through love become slaves to one another' (5:13). People began to see the Reformation as a bargain that made their lives easier, rather than a way of restoring integrity. They tired of any talk of helping their neighbors or caring for the poor."

"Your criticism reminds me of the writings of Dietrich Bonhoeffer and his concept of cheap grace," I interjected. "I wonder if you know him, Dr. Luther."[8]

"Yes, Lull," replied Luther, somewhat irritated at the interruption. "I know Bonhoeffer. That would be a long story—and not for today. But his phrase is a good one for the very frustration that I was already experiencing as I tried to preach to this city."

"Did you see this problem right away?" I asked.

"In part I did," answered Luther. "You can check out my Galatians commentary of 1519 and see the problem already reflected there.[9] What I did not bargain for was the special stubbornness of the people of this town. Oh, they were glad to see me when I came back in 1522 to restore order. They liked the fact that I helped to draw students to the university, which was good for the local merchants. But they quickly grew tired of my preaching, especially whenever I came to speak of the duties of Christians."

By now we had entered the outer building at the Luther house and moved into the courtyard where we sat facing the Augustinian monastery that became Luther's home.

"I remember your frustration with the towns-people in your plague treatise," I ventured.

"Yes, that's right. The issue was very clear in my mind by that time. It must have been 1528—and I know it was in the summer."

"Actually, Dr. Luther, I think it was 1527," I said, regretting these words as soon as they were out of my mouth.

But Luther laughed. "I think you're right, Lull. Imagine, you have to keep an eye on my memory. Well, perhaps it doesn't matter too much just which year it was. Outbreaks of the plague occurred from time to time, but we were especially hard hit that year. People were fleeing left and right, leaving dying neighbors with no one to care for them. 'Write something,' I was told, and while I could never figure out why people always thought I had the answer for this kind of practical thing, I did write about it—'Whether One May Flee from a Deadly Plague.'"[10]

I reached into my backpack and pulled out the Luther anthology. "Lo, I am with you always, Lull," he chuckled. "I suppose you want me to read something. Don't worry; it won't be the end of our talk this time. I still have a little more to say to you about this place. But perhaps you have a passage to suggest that captures my frustration with the people's indifference?"

I knew just where to point in my well-worn copy. So Luther read with great expression, as if he were rebuking the people this very day:

> This I well know, that if it were Christ or his mother who were laid low by illness, everybody would be so solicitous and would

gladly become a servant or helper. Everyone would want to be bold and fearless; nobody would flee but everyone would come running. And yet they don't hear what Christ himself says, "As you did it to one of the least, you did it to me" (Matt. 25:40). When he speaks of the greatest commandment he says, "The other commandment is like unto it, you shall love your neighbor as yourself" (Matt. 22:39). There you hear that the command to love your neighbor is equal to the command to love God, and that what you do or fail to do for your neighbor means doing the same to God. If you wish to serve Christ and wait on him, very well, you have your sick neighbor close at hand. Go to him and serve him, and you will surely find Christ in him, not outwardly but in his word. If you do not wish or care to serve your neighbor you can be sure that if Christ lay there instead you would not do so either and would let him lie there. Those are nothing but illusions on your part which puff you up with vain pride, namely, that you would really serve Christ if he were there in person.[11]

"Well, Lull," said Luther, "I'm glad you included that among my writings for your church today. I suspect it still needs saying."

It would have taken us far from Wittenberg to discuss how much North American Christians need to read this. I include myself. But instead I told Luther that this passage had come up in a recent debate that I had with another Lutheran theologian about Luther's understanding of community. I had argued that this was a central theme for Luther all the way through his career, a presupposition of his thought. My colleague thought that I was trying to make Luther modern or politically correct.

"What other evidence did you cite from me?" asked Luther, quite curious to hear about this.

I mentioned his 1519 treatise on the Lord's Supper in which he argues that those who share the Supper not only receive the great exchange of blessings and benefits from Christ, but also stand in a new relationship with each other. Soon I was paging through the anthology trying to find the passage in question. Now it was my turn to read:

> When you have partaken of this sacrament, therefore, or desire to partake of it, you must in turn share the misfortunes of the fellowship, as has been said. . . . Here your heart must go out in love and learn that this is a sacrament of love. As love and support are given to you, you in turn must render love and support to Christ and his needy ones. You must feel with sorrow all the dishonor done to Christ in his holy Word, all the misery of Christendom, all the unjust suffering of the innocent, with

which the world is everywhere filled to overflowing. You must fight, work, pray, and—if you cannot do more—have heart-felt sympathy. See, this is what it means to bear in your turn the misfortune and adversity of Christ and his saints.[12]

"Well chosen, Lull!" exclaimed Luther with a hearty pat on the back that showed me spirits also can make a substantial impact when they choose to do so. "I don't know what your colleague had in mind, and I can't imagine what it means to be polit-ically correct. I don't like the sound of it. But when you argue that I always saw the love of God and love of neighbor as inseparable, you are right. Perhaps some get confused because authentic love of neigh-bor is made possible by our first receiving God's great and gracious gift of love. But if people think that love of the neighbor is optional, there's some-thing wrong with our preaching and teaching.

"Nor did I ever suggest that Christian faith was a purely private matter, as some have written since in my name. You could also have used my cate-chisms here to good effect. We have discussed them before,[13] and I know that you retain a good knowledge of the basics—something I admire in any pastor or theologian. But I wonder how good your memory is. Can you recite the explanation to the Third Article of the Creed?"

I thought I could, because I always found its words so striking. So I began:

"I believe that I cannot by my own reason or strength believe in Jesus Christ my Lord or come to him. But the Holy Spirit has called me through the Gospel, enlightened me with gifts, sanctified and preserved me in true faith, just as that Spirit calls, gathers, enlightens, and sanctifies the whole Christian church on earth . . ."[14]

"Stop," said Luther. "Good enough. You see the point? The personal and the corporate belong together—the 'I' and the 'we.' The church always tends to neglect one pole or the other, but they belong together. No church without individual Christians, who enter the kingdom through baptism one at a time. But no individual Christians without the church. I had a lot to say critical of the church in my day, but I never thought we could do without it, especially the local community, the gathered congregation."

"And yet," I said, proceeding very carefully, "in the end you were very disappointed with this Wittenberg congregation. I read in your biographies, and in your own letters, of a time you were so mad that you refused to come home from your travels."

"Yes," said Luther, "it's true. It was the summer before I died—1545. I'm sure about this year! I was in Zeitz, feeling terrible. But I don't think that was the complete cause of my discouragement and reluctance to return. I really had come to fear that all my ministry here had been in vain. I wrote to Katie, telling her to sell our things, pack up, and come to join me. I hoped never to see Wittenberg again. I told her to tell Bugenhagen that she and he should say good-bye to everyone in my name. I wasn't even going back for that. Especially for that."[15]

"What was the effect of the letter?" I asked.

"It stirred up a terrible row. They sent a whole delegation out to meet with me, including John Frederick's personal physician. Bit by bit I made my way back home, finally convinced that it was probably for the best. In part they talked me into taking a more hopeful view. But in part I realized that there was nowhere else to go. The problems of Wittenberg are the problems of the human heart, and of the disparity between the gift of the gospel and the sad echo of even the best human response. I suspect you know what I'm talking about, Lull."

I was thinking of my own uneven life of faith and service. I was thinking of the disappointments that are always especially keen among people who see the gospel vision in a bright and clear way. I was thinking of congregations and seminaries in which I have, at times, been quite disappointed myself.

But now we were up and walking, and I suspected we were nearly done. "Well, Lull," said Luther, who was now cheerful again, "you have had four visits and you've heard almost my whole story. Now I must be going, but I think we are even. I've come to see you twice, and twice I've met you here in my old homes. We've covered everything but my death, and that, I happen to know, is written about at great length and all your questions could be taken to the books rather than to me personally."[16]

"There is one question they don't answer," I said. "You were brought back to Wittenberg for burial. Given what we were just discussing, about your relations with this town, was that all right?"

"From where I stand now," said Luther, "it doesn't make the least bit of difference. But where else were they going to put me? I had lived out my destiny in Wittenberg. It was the right place for me. If I have any regret, it is that they buried my Katie in Torgau.[17] I wish we were together, although in the ultimate and profound sense, of course we are."

"Will you read something before you go?" I asked.

"I did read something already, and at great length," said Luther, who nevertheless seemed willing. "But since this is to be our last conversation, of course. What will you have? Something from that fat Luther book?" He looked at my backpack.

But I pulled a piece of paper out of my pocket. "No," I said, "I have something else. This is your last sermon in Wittenberg. I thought something from that might be the way to close the book on these visits and on this city."

"Wonderful," said Luther. "Let me look for a minute and see what might do. Yes, I think this will be a good 'last word' from me on the subject of the Wittenbergers and my hopes for them."

> After baptism there still remains much of the old Adam. For, as we have often said, it is true that sin is forgiven in baptism, but we are not yet altogether clean, as is shown in the parable of the Samaritan, who carried the man wounded by robbers to an inn (Luke 10:30-37). He did not take care of him in such a way that he healed him at once, but rather bound up his wounds and poured on oil. The man who fell among robbers suffered two injuries. First, everything that he had was taken from him, he was robbed; and second, he was wounded, so that he was half-dead and would have died, if the Samaritan had not come to him. Adam fell among the robbers and implanted sin in us all. If Christ, the Samaritan, had not come, we should all have had to die. He it is who binds our wounds, carries us into the church and is now healing us. So we are now under the Physician's care. The sin, it is true, is wholly forgiven, but it has not been wholly purged. If the Holy Spirit is not ruling men, they become corrupt again, but the Holy Spirit must cleanse the wounds daily. Therefore this life is a hospital; the sin has really been forgiven, but it has not yet been healed.[18]

I was expecting Luther to vanish as soon as he finished reading, but instead he stood and shook my hand warmly. "We've talked mostly about me," said Luther. "We've hardly said anything about you. I know you have your struggles in your own life and a hard assignment as well in heading that school. Perhaps I'm not even quite healed yet, but still a little turned in on myself. Still, Lull, it's been a pleasure."

"Thank you, Dr. Luther," I said. "Sometimes the best help comes from outside, not only from God but from our neighbor. And in talking about yourself, you've been helping me." But before I finished this theological point—which I had been enjoying—he was gone, and I was left standing in the bright late-afternoon July sunshine in Lutherstadt Wittenberg.

The Final Visit
Weimar, Germany, July 1998

So that was that for visits with Luther. When we parted in Wittenberg, I had a sense that I had taken more than my share of his time. Of course, I was grateful for what I had learned, not only in substance, but also from his wonderful attitude. He was still Luther, but it was clear that eternity was having a beneficial effect. The capacity to laugh is often closely related to the understanding of grace, and Luther's laugh was far more prominent than I had found it in some of his late writings.

If I had one regret, it was that we had not had more time to talk about that final period—the five years or so before his death when he really did seem to be "old man Luther." I knew of fine writings from that period, especially his great commentary on the book of Genesis. But this was also the period of his harsh and very controversial writings about the Jews. We had talked about them briefly in his second visit, but still I wished there had been more. Perhaps it was just my imagination, but I felt that there had been a hint there of something more to discuss than we had covered in our session in Berkeley.

But I knew the dangers of wanting too much, like the fisherman in the fairy tale who kept going back to ask the magic fish for one grand thing after another until he and his wife ended up back in their humble cottage by the sea. It isn't exactly a Christian concept, but you could say that I didn't want to "press my luck." The day after my fourth conversation with Luther, we left Wittenberg for Weimar—the last stop on our Germany trip. My mind was turning to other matters.

There were some memories of the Reformation in Weimar, especially a collection of great paintings by Cranach and one especially wonderful painting—his memorial—in the town church in the Market Square. But we were actually in Weimar not so much on the trail of Luther as of other figures that interested us: people like the writers Goethe and Schiller, the musicians Bach and Franz Liszt. Weimar was a lovely old town associated with the failed experiment with democracy in Germany after the First World War—the Weimar Republic. And on the northern outskirts of the town was a terrible but momentous place that we hoped to visit if we could find the courage.

On the second morning of our stay in the lovely town, which is reemerging as one of Europe's great cultural cities, we got on a local bus and rode about six miles out to Buchenwald—that place where the Nazis built one of their terrible concentration camps in 1937. The numbers are beyond comprehension, even though this was far from the largest of such establishments. Almost a quarter million persons passed through the camp, and it is estimated that over 43,000 were killed outright or died in the subhuman conditions there. They built it here in part because this lovely cultural center Weimar was one of the strongest bastions of Nazi support.

Buchenwald is not a place to be visited lightly. We had to consider whether our need to see, to remember, and to pray would outweigh the horror of being there. I think it helped that the crowd on the day of our visit was very small. After some initial orientation, we made our way through the gate (with the bizarre inscription: "To each his own") and down into the area where rows of barracks once stood. The place is mostly open space now, and the unreality of what we were trying to comprehend was compounded by the beauty of the day and the view over the green and rolling Thuringian countryside.

We walked about, saying very little, but trying to help each other see what remains, to comprehend its grisly significance. We walked past the foundations of many barracks, past memorials to the dead, and eventually we made our way to the former storehouse that has been made into a museum of the camp. It is numbing and powerful to view the exhibits that trace the steady rise of the inhumanity that swept over Germany. Unfortunately, the blame must be shared by nations that cooperated eagerly with the extermination of the Jews, and with countries like the United States, which basically refused to take refugees even after they knew about the mass extermination.

The suffering of the Jewish people cries out the loudest, but we were aware of other groups as well. In the memorials and in the exhibits, we learned of others who were also special targets of the Nazi hatred, especially Poles, Czechs, gypsies, and homosexuals. In the museum, we found a few memorials of Christians who resisted all this and shared in the suffering of the victims, including Pastor Dietrich Bonhoeffer (who was held at Buchenwald from February until the beginning of April in 1945) and others like Pastor Paul Schneider.

By the time we came out of the museum it had started to rain. My wife was ready to go back to the hotel for a rest. We had promised to attend a concert by an American church choir in the town church of Saints Peter and Paul that evening.[1] I wanted to stay longer, even in the light rain. I wanted to walk to another part of the camp where Pastor Bonhoeffer had been a prisoner. So we said a quiet good-bye and I walked off in silence and sadness to do the little that one can do at such a place—show respect and vow to remember.

It was then that I met Luther again—to my surprise and to his obvious discomfort. I had been thinking of him, of course. Under the Nazis the terrible, angry, bitter writings against the Jews from his last years that had been largely forgotten in the archives achieved a kind of grizzly resurrection and new influence. Luther's works were dragged out of the library to add religious respectability to the Nazi hatred.

I knew that Luther was not alone in being anti-Jewish in his day. It is little comfort to say that other Reformers equaled the intensity of his views. But what Luther excelled in, here as elsewhere, was his power of expression. His greatness was his ability to articulate strongly that frustration with the church that was shared by so many others. Yet this was an ambiguous gift—one full of power to challenge authority or to proclaim the gospel memorably, but one that could fan terrible fires when he turned against his enemies.[2]

Such outbursts happened on more than one occasion. In the middle of the Peasants' War in 1525, when Luther's mediating attempts had been spurned by the peasants, he wrote an angry pamphlet urging the princes to "stab, smite, and slay."[3] These writings gained him the reputation of being the tool of the princes, even though earlier he had been critical of them. His concern for order in a situation where over 100,000 people died was forgotten, and what was remembered were angry words and an impression of indifference to injustice.

Luther's early writings about the Jews were anything but bitter. His treatise from 1523, "That Jesus Christ Was Born a Jew," urged Christians to consider their own responsibility for Jewish rejection of the gospel. Luther urged fair and kindly treatment of the Jews under any circumstances.[4] Luther's treatise stands out among the writings of this period as testimony to what might have been a new beginning for Christians and Jews together at the Reformation.

But later on, Luther became savagely critical of the Jews, perhaps spurred by current rumors and gossip. These late writings contain a degree of venom that shocked me when I first read his 1543 work, "On the Jews and Their Lies." In this book-length treatise, he argues that if the Jews finally will not accept Christ, then Christians would be justified in setting fire to synagogues, burning Jewish houses, destroying prayer books and religious writings, forbidding rabbis to teach, forcing hard labor, and finally expulsion from the land. These diatribes continued until the time of his death, even infecting the loving, grace-filled letters that he wrote to his wife from Eisleben in the last weeks of his life.[5]

You will be more interested in my interaction with Luther that day than in this summary of certain sad aspects of his career. But, to tell you the truth, our meeting at first was so abrupt, so awkward, that I was quite confused. And at this part of the visit, Luther had none of the jollity that was so characteristic of our other encounters. What became clear was that he had not come to see me this time by his free choice, but had been sent to be with me and to talk to me—to take up this unfinished business with me.

So we walked around the place for a time largely in silence as the soft rain fell. People kept their distance from each other here, except in the museum, where visitors tried to help each other understand what the exhibits meant, so we had little trouble being alone. When we came to the place where Bonhoeffer had been a prisoner, I got out my small travel Bible and read silently the words of Psalm 22—the great words repeated by Christ on the cross, words articulating the experience of being forsaken by God, full of sufferings and all alone. Yet this Good Friday psalm had new associations in this place:

> *For dogs are all around me,*
> *a company of evildoers encircles me.*
> *My hands and feet have shriveled;*
> *I can count all my bones.*
> *They stare and gloat over me;*
> *they divide my clothes among themselves,*
> *and for my clothing they cast lots.*
>
> —Psalm 22:16-18 (NRSV)

Luther waited at one side, saying nothing. Then we began to make our way back toward the gate and the bus stop. Luther proposed that we should walk back into Weimar together.

"I can't go all the way with you, Lull," he explained, "but I could go as far as the outskirts of Weimar. We clearly have matters to discuss. It's a long walk, but perhaps some exercise is best after an experience like this." His high voice was steady, but very sad.

"Have you been here before, Dr. Luther?" I asked.

"Oh, yes," said Luther heavily, "a great many times. There are many conversations that need to take place here. At first I did not think I could bear the grief of coming here—even in the blessedness of eternity. But it became clear that I had to go. And to help me, because I just could not comprehend it all and why it was any of my concern, I was assigned a guide. I think you know of him—Pastor Dietrich Bonhoeffer. You were visiting the place where he was a prisoner when I first began to walk with you back there."

Luther looked back over his shoulder, as I did. The camp now was dropping out of view. We left the historical site, continued on down the road, and turned onto a path through the woods. The rain was still falling, but very softly now. Had anyone noticed us, we must have been a sight, as I was wearing a bright yellow raincoat, and Luther was wrapped up in some kind of old-fashioned academic or ecclesiastical robe with a hood. But the way through the woods was deserted and gave us a long time to talk undisturbed.

"You did come to understand why you had been sent here?" I asked.

"Yes," replied Luther, "but it took some time. I had to comprehend the way in which my own writings became influential many centuries later, how they were used to make respectable what these Nazis were doing. I knew something in eternity of the horrors of your century, and even of the great suffering of the Jews, but I was slow to see any connection with me.

"Each generation must shoulder its own guilt, of course, from a human point of view. That's true even under a merciful and forgiving God. So one cannot blame Luther for the failure to love his neighbor in his own time and place. But do not seek fame or influence, Lull, or you may have much to answer for even to the tenth and the fifteenth generations."

"How did Bonhoeffer help you?" I asked, very much wishing that I could have been part of those conversations.

"You have heard about our ongoing Bible study in heaven, so you know that full understanding of the height and the depth and the breadth of God's ways comes slowly for us humans, even in that blessed place. But we often are sent to help each other come to a better understanding of some issues. I have sometimes been sent on such missions myself, but in this case, here at Buchenwald, I was the one in need. Bonhoeffer touched me initially with his great heart. I could see that he loved and cared about the Jews, the very people that I dismissed as the enemies of Christ. He always said it was a pleasure and an honor for him to be with me, but I felt in time that really it was just the other way around. A man so much younger became my teacher."

"But your views were quite set, Dr. Luther," I continued. "Can you share anything of the way that he worked with you?"

"We debated about the Bible," Luther reported, "and he opened my heart to new understandings of the Scriptures. Pray that it may happen for you some day, although I hope it will not be in such a painful way. I came to see that, like Paul—before his call to follow Jesus—I was so full of rage at those I considered wrong that I was dishonoring the very gospel that I wanted to serve."

"Perhaps the devil made you do it," I suggested, regretting the words as soon as they were out of my mouth.

"Yes, yes, exactly," said Luther, pounding vigorously on my back. "You say it lightly, but something like that must have happened. I was always on the lookout for him in all the obvious places. But his ways are subtle, Lull. Temptation so often lurks under the mask of righteousness, and especially self-righteousness. I knew that, and I even taught it. But I could not see where I was so vulnerable that it would also trap me."

"You had lots of company in your blindness," I offered quite tentatively.

Luther responded in irritation, "That is true, but hardly comforting or mitigating. In the end, each one must answer, must give an account of the talents given and the use made of them. Yes, Erasmus, Zwingli, and others of my time were also harsh against the Jews. Even your great Shakespeare made the Jew Shylock the center of a comedy in which Christians laugh cruelly at him.[6]

"But what of it? In my day I had opportunity to think more deeply of these things in my study of the Scriptures, but even when I saw something of the complexity of the counsels of God, actual encounters with Jews seemed to push all that aside. I could only see their rejection of Jesus as an insult to God."

"Perhaps one should leave God to care for God's own honor," I ventured.

"Exactly," said Luther, giving me another slug on the back. I wondered at this rate if I would be bruised by the time we got to Weimar. But he went on, "You remember how I taught in my catechisms that all sins are sins against the first commandment, failures to fear and love God with disastrous consequences? That was especially so for me. I should have seen that when I raged against the Jews of my time, I was acting just like the very church officials who persecuted me. Who made Luther the judge? In the end, I was misled by my professorship into thinking that such matters had been put in my jurisdiction. I even scolded princes for not expelling the Jews from their territory, forgetting that I had always warned against the church trying to engage in direct rule.[7] I needed to review the teaching of our Lord: 'Do not judge, so you may not be judged'" (Matt. 7:1).

"So what shall we say about the death of so many people, Dr. Luther?" I asked, sharing the question that any person of any faith must take away from Buchenwald.

The rain had stopped, but it was still wet and raw in the air. Luther shook his head. "Better to ask than to answer, Lull," he said, and I knew what he meant. No sound bite, no slogan, no Christian formula can be easily spoken with respect when the memory of those victims cries out to you. No revised theology that tries to take this great suffering into account can be spoken now, and perhaps not even for a long time to come. We walked on for a long time in silence. Then I asked about Weimar, as we were beginning to see the city in the distance, across the fields.

"I was here often," said Luther. "It was a favorite residence of Frederick the Wise's brother John, who eventually inherited his realm. The first visit I remember was when I was being sent to Augsburg to be interviewed by Cardinal Cajetan in 1518. What an arrogant monk I still was then, although I had scored quite a bull's-eye with my writings about indulgences! I came back here many, many times. I remember once especially when we all feared that Melanchthon was dying, and I came to try to pray him back to health. I think that was about 1540."

"I know that you preached here often," I said, reaching into my backpack.

"Yes," agreed Luther, "and with good results generally. I think those were the sermons on the great commandment to love God and to love your neighbor as yourself. It's a pretty basic message, but the whole Christian life is there if you unpack it in the right way."[8]

"Will you read from these sermons when we are at the end of this conversation?" I asked, for Luther had always done so. I was holding a copy of his Weimar sermons from 1522 that I had been carrying with me.

But he shook his head vigorously. "No, Lull," he said, "I will not read, and I will only walk on with you for a few minutes more. Soon this path rejoins the main road, and I will leave you to make your own way back to town. No more readings, and—unless I receive some surprising orders—no more visits. You have to make your own way now, even when the path is not clear. I have my own tasks, and there are other people who need my attention more than you do."

But still we walked on a little, so I felt the courage to ask another question, even though it was clear that we had not much more time. I wanted Luther to tell me about the great painting in the town church, which I had admired but not really understood. And that request seemed quite agreeable to him.

"I think you know, Lull," he began, "something about the difficulties in Wittenberg and Saxony after my death. The Emperor Charles V came marching in with his troops and defeated our princes, the Elector John Frederick and Philip of Hesse. The Catholic forces took control of the territory, and Charles threw John Frederick in prison. He told him that he would be put to death unless he cooperated in leading his people back into the Catholic fold.

"I wondered how John Frederick would do, Lull," Luther continued, "as he was a very nice man, and they are not always the best of leaders in troubled times. But he surprised everyone. He said that he would rather die than renounce the faith that had served him well. I think this refusal astonished Charles in the same way that my strong stand at Worms had done years before. He was not used to people saying 'No' to him. He left quite angry, but expecting that the Reformation was over, whatever this stubborn prince might do."

"But they were not successful," I said, "at least from what I know."

"Yes," said Luther, smiling for the first time during that visit. "The gospel had taken pretty deep root. The Catholic side offered to allow the marriage of priests and communion to the laity of both bread and wine, but it was far too late for such surface changes to suffice. The Prince held firm—even through years in prison—and the people did too."

"Some say Melanchthon went too far in cooperating with the Interim," I began, but Luther interrupted me.

"I just hate all these folks who are so correct that they can judge people from a great distance and after many centuries. How much do they know about it? Were they there? You Lutherans, as you call yourselves, seem to be the biggest gossips of any Christian group in the world. It was a hard time, and people felt their way as best they could. Philipp could always see hope ahead and possibility, just as I tended to expect the worst. It was a time when my close friends differed deeply, but I was not there and neither were you. It's hard to imagine we would have done much better."

"But the picture in the Weimar church?" I asked, somewhat uncomfortable with the drift of this discussion and fearing that Luther would disappear before we got to the end of the story. Instead we sat down together on a tree trunk. The path we had been walking ended at the road only about fifty yards ahead, but Luther clearly wanted time to finish his story.

"Well, Lull," continued Luther, "I've said before that Lucas Cranach the painter was the one witness to the whole saga of the Reformation, from the very beginnings in Wittenberg to the hard times after my death. When John Frederick was finally released from prison, he was given only this small area around Weimar to rule, a little remnant of the once great territory of Electoral Saxony. But Lucas followed him here. You can see his grand house on one of the fine squares. And after John Frederick died, and knowing that his own death was near, Lucas began to paint that great scene of Christ crucified as a memorial to all of us. His son Lucas finished it after his death.

"You have seen it?" Luther asked. I nodded and he continued.

"Then you remember that at the foot of the cross stands the artist himself, between John the Baptist and me! I must say, I liked that when I first saw it. I hope I was a kind of John the Baptist—strong words and all. And the striking thing in the picture is the blood of Christ falling on Lucas's head. I think of it as the last great Reformation confession—worthy in its own way to stand with the Augsburg Confession and my catechisms."

"I admired all that in the painting," I reported. "But in our day we find the blood falling on the head of the artist a little too disturbing. Perhaps there's been too much blood in our century," I said in an attempted explanation for my uneasiness with the subject matter.[9]

"Yes," said Luther, "what you say is true. Too much blood in your century and in every century. Mine as well." And with that he began to walk away. "But take care, Lull," he added, looking back at me over his shoulder as he walked away, "that you don't become too sophisticated for the love of Jesus and the mercy of God. What we've seen today ought to drive you modern people to your knees."

I think it was supposed to be Luther's exit line, but I panicked and went running after him, crying, "Dr. Luther, don't go. Wait."

"Look, Lull," he said, turning toward me, "now I really must go. The sun is almost out again, although this day will be basically overcast right to the end. Go back to your hotel. And don't get addicted to these conversations. You have better things to do. But if you can't live without them, you can always make them up. You know enough now to be able to do it yourself."

And then he was gone, and I was on the road just outside the north end of Weimar. I had a city bus pass and, deciding that I had walked enough that day, I took the next bus back to town. Soon I was back at our hotel, having my own nap before the evening concert.

We walked to the Market Church in the rain that night, and the music was wonderful. It was fun to watch Germans listening to Americans performing Bach's great Cantata No. 80, which is itself based on Luther's hymn, "A Mighty Fortress Is Our God." After the service, we greeted several acquaintances who were present and very surprised to run into us so far from home. While my wife continued to talk with them, I wandered away for a last close look at the altar painting.

And there was the scene that Luther and I had discussed. On the left, John Frederick and his wife, Sybil, who died by the time that the picture was finished, were shown kneeling. On the right were their three surviving sons, who paid for it. In the great central panel, Christ was stretched out on the cross, with blood from his side arcing onto the head of Lucas Cranach the Elder, who stood in the bottom right between the Baptist and Luther. In the background were various biblical scenes, including the Garden of Eden and the brass serpent on the pole erected by Moses in the wilderness. But I could not make out one key scene.

Talking to myself, as I so often do when I think the coast is clear, I said, "I wonder what that beast is flying through the air in the top of the picture. I'd better get out my glasses. I can't tell if it's a dragon or an angel."

"Good heavens, Lull," came the answer, "that's

an angel. Not that Lucas Cranach couldn't paint a fine dragon on demand. But that's the angel and the shepherds of Bethlehem, a story that I think you must know quite well."[10]

I looked around but there was no sign of Luther at all. "Hmm," I thought. "Perhaps this is what he was talking about when he left this afternoon." So I answered, "Well in any case it's a handsome picture of you, Dr. Luther."

"Do you think so?" the voice said, sounding quite interested. "I suppose it somewhat resembles the way I looked at the end. But really, Lull, I think I look a little old there. Was I ever that heavy? Is that how you folks today think of me? Not that it matters, after all, where I am now."

Just then my wife came up and pulled on my sleeve. She pointed out that people were noticing my mumbling over in the corner of the church, and that this might not be the best image for a seminary president. "Were you talking to yourself?" she asked.

"Yes and no. It's more complicated than you might imagine," I said, taking her arm as we walked toward the door of the church. "I'll tell you about it when we get back to the hotel."

In Place of a Conversation with Katherine von Bora

I've never been lucky enough to have a conversation with Katherine von Bora, better known to the world as Mrs. Martin Luther. I'd love to know her version of all these events. But such conversations cannot be faked; they happen or they don't. So, in order that she might in some way be present in the book, and because it is published in the year of her 500th birthday, this sermon in her honor is attached to my conversations with her husband.

She is important beyond the fact that she shared the last two decades of Luther's life. When she left the convent and came to Wittenberg to take up life in the world, she was representative of many women and men who heard the call of the Reformation to a new form of discipleship, living out one's ministry in daily life in the world. It appears that this was not much easier than life in the religious community had been. But we are all heirs of her and of Martin. We are descendants of the Reformation who continue to struggle with the cost of discipleship and with its contents in the perplexities of life in the modern world.

KATHERINE VON BORA LUTHER: DISCIPLE

A sermon in honor of her 500th birthday
January 31, 1999
St. Mark's Lutheran Church, San Francisco

Blessed are you when people revile you and persecute you and utter all kinds of evil against you falsely, on my account. Rejoice and be glad, for your reward is great in heaven, for in the same way they persecuted the prophets who were before you. (vs.11-12)

Grace and peace to you from God the Father of our Lord Jesus Christ in the Holy Spirit.

Five hundred years ago last Friday, a young woman was born in a noble family in Germany. Such a background might have indicated prospects for a pleasant life, but this did not happen for several reasons. Her family, though aristocratic, was recently impoverished. Then her mother died when she was very young. A stepmother arrived and, at age five, the young girl was sent away from home for schooling in a convent. By age ten she was moved to another religious community for women with the intention that she would become a nun. This became official when she was sixteen, as Katherine von Bora took the vows of chastity, poverty, and obedience, expecting to live in that same quiet Cistercian community for the rest of her life. Her aunt Lena was a nun there, having been destined for the same vocation by the same family years earlier.

We know that religious communities were one of the few arenas in the Middle Ages in which Christian women could achieve leadership. Katherine was given an unusual amount of education for a woman in those days. She learned to read—a new skill for non-priests that was sweeping Europe at the time—and she even learned Latin. But reading can lead to complications. A few years later, she and the other sisters of the Nimbschen convent began reading the theological works of their Saxon neighbor, the monk Martin Luther.

No doubt many persons found happiness and peace with God in such religious communities. Many do to this day. But others, like Katherine, were there not from free consent, but by a decision made for them at an early age. This woman and eleven of her sisters wanted to leave. A local farmer who had become a supporter of the Reformation and who had a daughter among the group, made regular delivery of supplies to the convent.

On Easter Eve of 1523, he dropped off some barrels of herring for the feast the next day. It is told that the twelve women hid themselves in herring barrels to escape. In any case, they all arrived in Wittenberg and were brought to Martin Luther's personal attention on the Tuesday after Easter. Here they were, inspired by his writings to leave their old life. Now he was expected to find a new one for them.

You might wonder why they had to go to all this trouble to escape. Many monks and nuns simply walked away from their communities and entered the world. But it happened that these nuns lived in a part of Germany that was ruled by Luther's archenemy, Duke George of Saxony. He was not going to have any Reformation nonsense in his territory, whatever might be taking place in the neighboring realm of his cousin, Frederick the Wise. Promises were promises, and nuns and monks and priests could just sit still and get over any doubts they were having. But at this time the new ideas—like Christian freedom and service of the neighbor in daily life were sweeping powerfully among the people, even to the convent in Nimbschen from which Katherine escaped.

Three of the twelve nuns were able to go back to their families of origin, but nine had nowhere to go. Luther found places for them to live with respectable families in Wittenberg. Now Katherine's luck began to change. She was placed in the household of Lucas and Barbara Cranach; Cranach was the town painter, the druggist, and a very close friend of Professor Martin Luther.

Every attempt was made to get these young women married. Katherine was twenty-four and reasonably attractive. We know that the King of Denmark, a frequent visitor to Wittenberg, was impressed enough with her to give her a ring as a present. But none of the proposed matches worked out. Finally, she told Luther's friend, Professor Amsdorf, that she would be willing to marry either him or Dr. Luther himself.[1]

What did Luther think of such a proposal? By this time, many nuns and priests and monks had married and Luther had supported them vigorously. But he had not taken the step himself for several reasons. He knew that people would say that the Reformation was really all about sex if he—its most public leader—were to marry. But there was an even more serious obstacle. Luther was a man who had been condemned to death by the Emperor Charles V. At any point Imperial troops could come sweeping into Wittenberg, seize him, and burn him at the stake immediately or send him off to Rome for death there. How could such an outlaw in good conscience take a wife or begin a family?

But the idea stuck in his mind that he, himself, might eventually marry. He visited his parents in the spring of 1525 and found them very excited about the possibility. His old prince, the always cautious Frederick the Wise, had died a few months earlier, and Luther now had unconditional support from the new elector, Duke John. So, despite the opposition of some friends, Martin Luther, the miner's son and former monk, and Katherine von Bora, the nobleman's daughter and former nun, were betrothed on June 13, 1525, and married in great festivity two weeks later.[2] The farmer who arranged the nuns' escape and Luther's parents were among the guests. Cranach painted their pictures along with dual portraits of the wedding couple.

Since all of this has sounded like a fairy tale so far, from the stepmother to the escape in herring barrels to the King of Denmark's ring, you will probably want to know whether they lived happily ever after. We'll come to that in a few minutes. But first I want you to think about the change in Katherine's life from nun to wife, from serving God in the convent in celibacy to serving God in Wittenberg in family life.

She had been given by her family to the church, with the understanding that was common at that time: some persons should take the faith very seriously so that they could intercede on behalf of the larger Christian community.

All Christians were baptized, to be sure, but the monks and priests and nuns like Katherine were the ones who were expected to go all the way with following Jesus. They were expected to live the Beatitudes (which were read to us this morning). How often she must have heard them in her cloister, and been taught to think that she and her sisters were the very ones who were specially called to be meek, to hunger for righteousness, to be merciful, to be peacemakers.

But Luther's interpretation of the Bible was spelling out another way, another understanding. He taught that the Pentecost promise of the gift of the Spirit to all—young and old, men and women—meant that all persons had been called to be priests, to be evangelists, to be servants of Christ. He understood the beatitudes not as the code of the Christian elite, but as the announcement of God of the surprising and wonderful ways of the coming kingdom with which all disciples needed to ally themselves. He saw them as applying to all Christians, just as much to the housewife in town as to the nun in the cloister.

It was no doubt thrilling to escape from the strict discipline of the convent, to breathe more freely, to have more control of one's own destiny. All who have struggled for freedom and identity in our own lives can understand why Katherine did what she did, and we cheer for her. But she was also a pioneer of the new Reformation understanding of the Christian life that continues right down to our own time. All Christians are called to discipleship. But better than the values of chastity, poverty, and obedience are the gospel values of faith, hope, and love—which Christ intends us to live out in the disciplines and tasks of everyday life, in the service of our neighbors.

Did they live happily ever after? Yes and no. It was Katherine's lot to pass the rest of her life as the wife, and then as the widow, of the most famous

Christian of her time—Dr. Martin Luther. And how did that go? It seems clear that Luther at least was not particularly in love when they got married; he took the step to make a theological point and to solve a problem—what to do with Katherine. But thanks to the grace and wonderful sense of humor of God, Luther most definitely came in time to be in love. We are saddened not to know Katherine's version of things, as none of her letters have survived. But we can see from Luther's letters, and from other contemporary accounts, that they were happy together, even if I can't assure you that they lived happily ever after. He called her "his theologian" and even "the morning star of Wittenberg."

There were both joys and sorrows in their family life. Six children were born to them—three sons and three daughters. One daughter died in infancy, and another—the beloved Magdalena—caused her parents deep and lasting grief when she died at age thirteen. The oldest son was pushed into the university at too young an age, before he was ready, and had a terrible struggle with his father's shadow. But they were, for all that, a close and loving family.

There were both joys and sorrows in Katherine's daily work. No longer was it her chief task to pray the psalms. Now she was expected to manage the huge Luther household, including not only her husband and those children, but other relatives (including her Aunt Lena from the convent who came to live with them in the sprawling former Augustinian monastery), many visitors, some of them nobility, and many students. The Luthers ran a student hostel to help pay their bills. Martin's own demanding work schedule meant, of course, that Katherine ran the hostel herself, including collecting the fees. Luther was so busy being Luther.

She was a hard worker and a good manager, the tough individual that every family needs to have somewhere, who could say no, set limits, and see that the bills were paid. She became an excellent farmer and a somewhat successful brewer of beer. When Luther chided her to read the Bible more, she told him she had pretty much mastered the Bible in the convent but now had to figure out how to live the Bible. This makes her an excellent role model for us modern Christians who try to live out our discipleship in the dilemmas and pressures of everyday life.

There were many happy moments in their years together—banquets and celebrations and much making of music. The King of Denmark sent a barrel of herring every year. But there were many sorrows, deaths, and illnesses—including Luther's chronic poor health for most of the twenty years that they were married. And there was active hostility. A loyal servant of Duke George—Luther's enemy and now Katherine's—wrote a pamphlet attacking her directly, claiming that she was a "little rat servant," a "dancing girl," Luther's mistress, and one who had led many nuns astray. Katherine knew a great deal about what our Lord describes as the time "when people revile you and persecute you and utter all kinds of evil against you falsely on my account."

Yet in all of this she was able to "rejoice and be glad." Luther feared that she would suffer after his death, and he was right. It was not only the loss of this extraordinary companion that made her mourn, but the troops of the emperor swept into Wittenberg the year after Luther died and attempted to bring back the old religion by force. Her patron, Duke John Frederick, was thrown into prison and threatened with death. Luther's followers began quarreling about who was really Lutheran, a tradition that continues to this day. Katherine had to leave Wittenberg more than once, to scramble for money to feed and educate her children.

Finally, things seemed to be settling down, and she was able to go home, but soon the plague swept through Wittenberg and she had to flee to the nearby city of Torgau. She was injured in an accident when a wagon turned over on her way into that city and died there a few months later in December of 1552—six years after the death of her husband. She died confessing faith in Christ—the one constant in her life in the convent and in Wittenberg—as an old Catholic and a new Lutheran. She is reported to have said on her deathbed, "I will stick to Christ as a burr sticks to a topcoat."

Our Lord Jesus tells us that those whom the world pities, or even despises, are the blessed, the happy, the fortunate. Katherine, who was proud, and energetic, and sharp-tongued, may not have been among the meek. But she knew a lot about several other beatitudes. She had many occasions to mourn, she clearly hungered and thirsted for righteousness, she was a peacemaker—generally—in contrast to her fiery husband, and we know that she was one against whom people spoke all kinds of evil.

But the promise of the coming kingdom and faith in the one who proclaimed it sustained her through good times and bad. A year before Luther died, he was so discouraged with how little the Reformation had accomplished in Wittenberg that he wrote to Katie and told her to pack her things and come join him. They would find somewhere else to live, somewhere where the gospel might take better root, where the attitude of the people was less selfish and indifferent to the poor and the needy.

She helped talk him into coming back home because, from such disappointment, in ourselves and in our fellow Christians, there is no running away. The task of living the life of the coming kingdom always surpasses the best vows we make, the most loving families, the best preaching and worship. But this too is covered by the promise of the gospel. For disciples look not to our own wisdom or strength, but to a kingdom that comes from beyond us and all too often despite us.

As we walk that discipleship road in our own time, as we experience both joy and sorrow, both reformation and disappointment, we give thanks to God not only for teachers like Martin Luther, but also that there have been ordinary saints like the extraordinary Katherine von Bora Luther. May this brief remembrance of her 500th birthday spur us to rejoice and be glad, to know that we are blessed, to serve others in our station in life, and to take up again the challenge of discipleship in the world of everyday.

The peace of God that passes all understanding keep your hearts and minds in Christ Jesus our Lord.

APPENDIX I
RESOURCES FOR HAVING YOUR OWN CONVERSATION WITH LUTHER

There is a basic decision at the beginning of any serious study of Luther: whether to *read* him or whether to *read about* him. The person who gets really interested in Luther will want to do both.

But my complaint for years has been that there has been too much reading about Luther and not enough reading of him. The vibrant and bracing encounter that is part of any conversation with Luther is always muted in any book about him, even this one. Biographies of Luther have the almost inescapable problem noted in attempted biographies of Jesus of sounding too much like the life of the author himself or herself. This book—*My Conversations with Martin Luther*—would have its greatest potential value if it prodded the person who reads it to want to read Luther directly.

I.

The reader of this book will find a comfortable bridge for further study in the anthology that I edited a decade ago, one that has been referred to often in the footnotes of this book: Timothy F. Lull, editor, *Martin Luther's Basic Theological Writings* (Minneapolis: Fortress, 1989). The book was put together as a text for college and seminary students who can be frustrated that Luther's most important writings are scattered among the fifty-five volumes of the American Edition. It includes thirty-one documents, almost all of them complete treatises (to help Luther speak for himself without editorial "improvement"). General readers have made good use of the book when they did not feel obligated to read "straight through" but followed their own interests.

An older anthology, widely available and still quite valuable, is John Dillenberger, editor, *Martin Luther: Selections from his Writings* (Garden City, N.Y.: Doubleday, 1961). This has about one-third of the same material that is in the Lull anthology, although some of the documents are from translations older than the American Edition. It contains less material on Luther's developed view of the sacraments and ecclesiology (key issues in recent ecumenical theology) than the Lull volume, but does have excellent selections from Luther's "Lectures on Galatians" (1531) and "To the Christian Nobility of Germany" (1520), which are not in the Lull edition.

A third anthology, by Eric Gritsch, collected Luther's writings in a volume aimed at Roman Catholic readers: *Martin Luther—Faith, Christ and the Gospel* (Hyde Park, N.Y.: New City Press, 1996). This book contains excerpts thematically selected, including Luther's commentaries on the flood story from Genesis, on the Magnificat, and on the Sermon on the Mount. It is very general reader-friendly.

Martin Marty edited a small volume of excerpts from Luther's "Sermon on the Mount": *The Place of Trust* (San Francisco: Harper and Row, 1983).

The full range of Luther's thought is found in the fifty-five volumes of the American Edition. The first thirty are from Concordia Publishing House; the last twenty-five are from Fortress Press. Especially good volumes for the general reader include:

Volume 1: *Lectures on Genesis 1–5* (1535–36) and volume 21: *The Sermon on the Mount* (1530) and *The Magnificat* (1521). These give splendid samples of Luther's chief vocation, that of biblical professor. The commentary on Mary's Song (the Magnificat of Luke 1:46-55) is not only a view of Luther's positive estimating of the Virgin Mary, but is also a key to his theology of the cross, which explores the hidden and surprising ways that God works in the world.

Volumes 42–43: *Devotional Writings* 1 and 2. These volumes show that Luther devoted lifelong attention to forms of prayer and devotion that would replace (and in many cases build on) the spirituality of the monasteries that he had left behind.

Volumes 48–50: *Luther's Letters* 1, 2, and 3. These allow the reader to follow Luther's life in detail and in his own words, but also make for excellent browsing as one sees his different styles in writing to his princes, his friends, his wife, his parents, and his children.

Volume 51: *Sermons* 1. This gives a sense of the diversity of topics and styles in Luther's preaching and provides another overview of his whole life's work.

One of the most attractive presentations of Luther as pastor is found in a book edited by Theodore Tappert, *Luther: Letters of Spiritual Counsel* (Philadelphia: Westminster, 1955). Tappert includes a great deal of material, which is nowhere else available in English, and shows Luther's creativity and sometimes surprising tenderness in responding to the whole range of pastoral issues and personal difficulties of his day. This valuable resource, long out of print, has recently been reissued by Regent College, Bellingham, Washington.

II.

In studying the life of Luther, one has an abundance of good options and some decisions about how current and how detailed an approach one wants. The classic in English for this century was Roland Bainton, *Here I Stand: A Life of Martin Luther* (Nashville: Abingdon, 1950—with many paperback editions subsequently). No one has greater narrative power, and Bainton drew on all the scholarship available to him. It is still much worth reading.

However, half a century later, after new scholarly developments, and after a great ecumenical shift, Luther's story needs telling in other ways. An intentional updating of Bainton and discussion of both positive and problematic themes in Luther's theology is found in Eric Gritsch, *Martin—God's Court Jester* (Philadelphia: Fortress, 1983—and now reprinted by Sigler Press). James Kittleson's *Luther: The Reformer* (Minneapolis: Augsburg, 1986) is also very readable and an up-to-date choice that presents Luther's life taking into account more recent research.

Two out-of-print books that may be available in church libraries are also recommended: James Atkinson, *Martin Luther and the Birth of Protestantism* (Baltimore: Penguin paper, 1968), and James Nestigen, *Martin Luther: His Life and Teaching* (Philadelphia: Fortress, 1982). Another older book that still gives the clearest account of Luther's early years is Gordon Rupp, *Luther's Progress to the Diet of Worms* (New York: Harper, paper, 1964). The next period is covered in Martin Bornkamm's *Luther in Mid-Career* (Philadelphia: Fortress, 1983), translated by the late E. Theodore Bachmann.

The more serious reader now has all the detail one could ever wish for in Martin Brecht's three-volume biography of Luther, which draws on the best German and international research from the past half-century. These are: *Martin Luther: His Road to Reformation 1483–1521* (Philadelphia: Fortress, 1985), *Martin Luther: Shaping and Defining the Reformation 1521–32* (Philadelphia: Fortress, 1990), and *Martin Luther: The Preservation of the Church: 1532–46* (Minneapolis: Fortress, 1993). All three volumes are now available in paperback editions. Brecht is very readable, thanks to the fine translation of the late James Schaaf, although the story is inevitably quite detailed and confusing even in the best of presentations, which Brecht's surely is. Church and public libraries really should have this resource available, which surpasses all the one-volume treatments.

The most exciting book about Luther since Bainton, challenging both scholarly and popular ways of reading, is Heiko Oberman's *Luther: Man between God and the Devil* (New Haven: Yale University Press, 1989—a translation of the original German work from 1982—with paperback reprints). Oberman uses his lifetime of scholarly expertise to issue a clear warning about the dangers of modernizing Luther—a demonstration of how difficult it really is to have a conversation with him. His book stands, of course, as a message about the perils in an enterprise like *My Conversations with Martin Luther*, as I am well aware. It is hard to escape being deeply influenced by this revisionist account, one that suggests that Luther's "preoccupation with the devil" stands at the very heart of his witness and is relevant to skeptical modern readers. This volume requires a little harder work than some of the others listed above, but it can be very deeply rewarding, especially for those who already know the basic story.

Someday soon I hope we'll have more resources in English on Luther's friends (Melanchthon, about whom there is a growing literature, Bugenhagen, Jonas, Cranach, Amsdorf, and the others who really functioned as a team during Luther's lifetime). Sometime soon there should also be more about Katherine von Bora and Luther's family. In the meantime, I still recommend the essay about her in Roland Bainton's *Women of the Reformation in Germany and Italy* (Boston: Beacon, 1971).

III.

Once one has read some Luther and read about Luther, a vast array of books offer help with more specialized topics, from understanding his theology to the wider context of his times. Especially helpful and clear on the theology is Gerhard Forde, *Where God Meets Man* (Minneapolis: Augsburg, 1972). A more recent Forde volume takes up what I consider Luther's greatest (and most elusive) theological achievement—his theology of the cross: *On Being a Theologian of the Cross* (Grand Rapids: Eerdmans, 1997).

The implications of Luther for cultures and contexts beyond the North Atlantic are a rich field of current study. One of the best books from this study is by a Brazilian Lutheran theologian who is well grounded in Luther and sympathetic to the themes of liberation theology: Walter Altmann, *Luther and Liberation* (Minneapolis: Fortress, 1992). It is one of the finest examples of a conversation with Luther that I know.

The development of Lutheranism from Luther's thought and other sources is clearly and popularly presented in Eric Gritsch's *Fortress Introduction to Lutheranism* (Minneapolis: Fortress, 1994). A recent account of the whole Reformation history, sensitive to ecumenical and women's concerns and drawing on recent work in the social history of the Reformation, is Carter Lindberg, *The European Reformations* (Cambridge, Mass.: Blackwell, 1996). Mark Edwards has written several fine books on Luther; the most recent will interest many general readers: *Printing, Propaganda and Martin Luther* (Berkeley: University of California Press, 1994).

It is surprisingly hard to find good books on the artist Lucas Cranach, his family, his Reformation paintings, and his relations with Luther. But now a splendid treatment is available in John Dillenberger, *Images and Relics: Theological Perceptions and Visual Images in Sixteenth Century Europe* (New York: Oxford, 1999), with a long chapter on Cranach and many fine illustrations.

Beyond the budget of most individuals, but quite appropriate for any good church or public library collection, is an outstanding new four-volume reference work that answers almost every question imaginable about this period: Hans J. Hillerbrand of Duke University and an all-star team of Reformation historians have produced *The Oxford Encyclopedia of the Reformation* (New York: Oxford, 1996). Anyone who has read this book with pleasure will greatly enjoy browsing around the many topics addressed in detail in the encyclopedia, from Luther and Katherine themselves (fine summaries by Martin Brecht) to women in the Reformation; to Luther's friends; to the liturgical wars of the 16th century; or to the tragic and complex history of Christians and Jews in this period.

A final specialized volume is indispensable for anyone who goes to Germany to see the Luther places. It is a detailed guide to almost all the important, or even marginal places, in Luther's life: Wolfgang Hoffmann, *Luther: A Practical Travel Guide* (Wernigerode: Schmidt-Buch-Verlag, 1995). It is hard to obtain in America but can be found at many souvenir shops in Germany. With it you can not only have conversations with Luther, but take walks with him as well.

Appendix II
DECLARATION OF THE ELCA TO THE JEWISH COMMUNITY

The Church Council of the Evangelical Lutheran Church in America on April 18, 1994, adopted the following document as a statement on Lutheran-Jewish relations:

In the long history of Christianity there exists no more tragic development than the treatment accorded the Jewish people on the part of Christian believers. Very few Christian communities of faith were able to escape the contagion of anti-Judaism and its modern successor, anti-Semitism. Lutherans belonging to the Lutheran World Federation and the Evangelical Lutheran Church in America feel a special burden in this regard because of certain elements in the legacy of the reformer Martin Luther and the catastrophes, including the Holocaust of the twentieth century, suffered by Jews in places where the Lutheran churches were strongly represented.

The Lutheran communion of faith is linked by name and heritage to the memory of Martin Luther, teacher and reformer. Honoring his name in our own, we recall his bold stand for truth, his earthy and sublime words of wisdom, and above all his witness to God's saving Word. Luther proclaimed a gospel for people as we really are, bidding us to trust a grace sufficient to reach our deepest shames and address the most tragic truths.

In the spirit of that truth-telling, we who bear his name and heritage must with pain acknowledge also Luther's anti-Judaic diatribes and the violent recommendations of his later writings against the Jews. As did many of Luther's own companions in the sixteenth century, we reject this violent invective, and yet more do we express our deep and abiding sorrow over its tragic effects on subsequent generations. In concert with the Lutheran World Federation, we particularly deplore the appropriation of Luther's words by modern anti-Semites for the teaching of hatred toward Judaism or toward the Jewish people in our day.

Grieving the complicity of our own tradition in this history of hatred, moreover, we express our urgent desire to live out our faith in Jesus Christ with love and respect for the Jewish people. We recognize in anti-Semitism a contradiction and an affront to the Gospel, a violation of our hope and calling, and we pledge this church to oppose the deadly working of such bigotry, both within our own circles and in the society around us. Finally, we pray for the continued blessing of the Blessed One upon the increasing cooperation and understanding between Lutheran Christians and the Jewish community.

ACKNOWLEDGMENTS

I am grateful for speaking invitations where I've been able to develop much of the material in this book, including those from the Rocky Mountain, Pacifica, Southern California West and Southwest Washington Synod Assemblies and the New England and the Southeastern Synod Pastoral Convocations. I believe that it was Bishop Allan C. Bjornberg who first pressed me to try this kind of presentation. An early version was presented at the Sittler Symposium in 1994. The Lutheran Campus Ministry at the University of Arizona also heard a portion of this work in progress as did Augustana Lutheran Church in Denver.

I've been stimulated by my students in my classes on Luther and Lutheranism during the past decade at Pacific Lutheran Theology Seminary and by colleagues on the "Lutheranism team," including Michael Aune, Ted Peters, Martha Stortz, and Jane Strohl—all of us working in an optimal climate for Luther studies here that is the legacy of Professor Emeritus Robert Goeser, who continues to teach this material superbly. Professors Stortz and Strohl each read the manuscript with helpful suggestions, but the unusual nature of the project is in no way to be blamed on them.

Acknowledgments

Special deep thanks goes to the participants in the annual Luther Seminars at the Graduate Theological Union Summer School. Over our five sessions together we have had truly memorable dealings with Luther. I hope they will see our work reflected in these conversations.

I'm aware that this book would never have been written without enthusiasm and also pressure from Augsburg Fortress, especially its Editorial Director, Henry French, an old colleague. It has been delightful to work with him in a new way. Ronald Klug was a sympathetic but critical editor—every author's dream. Timothy W. Larson was a delightful and speedy production editor.

I should especially like to thank my wonderful administrative assistant, Sharon Gruebmeyer, for extensive assistance with this project.

The International Lutheran Student Center in London and its warden, Mr. David Ward, provided, once again, a splendid home away from home for planning and the initial writing.

Bishop H. George Anderson gave the project a helpful nudge at a moment of this author's greatest discouragement.

The particular shape of the book owes everything to a three-week visit to Germany in the summer of 1998. Then, as for the last three decades of my life, I had the advantage of experiencing the world in the exquisite company of Mary-Carlton Lull. Thanks to her for proposing the trip. The idea for the book came from our reading in those weeks of the old classic by Goethe's young associate, J. P. Eckermann's *Conversations with Goethe*.

I also thank her—along with two members of my family, our son, Christopher R. C. Lull, and my sister, Pastor Patricia J. Lull—for improvements that resulted from their reading of the manuscript.

What storytelling abilities I have were nourished by my father, Raymond R. Lull, who was a factory worker who also taught Sunday school for more than forty years. He knew that half the work of teaching is catching and keeping the interest of students. He and my mother, Ruth Cole Lull, found their faith to be a matter of deep importance for their daily lives. I've thought of them often during my work on this project and tried to ask Luther the questions that they would have posed were he sitting at their kitchen table. I have hoped that our sons and our nieces and nephews might catch a glimpse here, even indirectly, of why that entire older generation so loved their Lutheran tradition.

The book is dedicated to the Lutherans of New England among whom my pastoral and theological identity was nourished and who are good friends to this day. Though at times they worry about being small or marginal, for the most part they go on being the church with splendid hope and courage. They have a deep but not defensive Lutheran identity—which I am persuaded will be the only kind of viable Lutheranism for the future.

In 1993, some of them led the revolt—along with the Lutherans from Northeast Pennsylvania—from the floor to the churchwide assembly of the Evangelical Lutheran Church in America in demanding a statement that would clarify that Luther's teachings on the Jews have no influence, and are in fact repudiated, by our church today. It was a great moment of overcoming bureaucratic inertia when they were successful.

The persons I cherish are too numerous to name individually, but I think especially of Rev. Richard E. Koenig, Dean Richard L. Thulin, Professor George A. Lindbeck, the late Professor Sydney E. Ahlstrom, Rev. Paul T. Lindstrom, Rev. Robert L. Griesse, Rev. Arthur W. von Au, Rev. Frederick P. Auman Jr., Rev. Jack R. Stevens, Mr. Donald G. Johnson, and the pastors (especially Rev. Joseph L. Carucci and Rev. Leslie R. Swenson) and members of Grace Lutheran Church, Needham, Massachusetts. They took a chance on me long ago (when some wondered whether my theological education was "properly Lutheran"). Former bishops Eugene A. Brodeen and Harold R. Wimmer deserve much credit for this gamble. I've been grateful ever since, not only for that opportunity, but that it fell to me to learn to do pastoral ministry from them and among these New Englanders.

—Timothy F. Lull
London and Berkeley
1999

NOTES

Chapter 1

1. Martin Luther, "Preface to the New Testament" (1522—revised 1546) in Timothy F. Lull, ed., *Martin Luther's Basic Theological Writings* (Minneapolis: Fortress, 1989), p. 117.

2. For a fuller discussion of Luther and the peasants, see chapter 4; for Luther and the Jews, see the conversation in chapter 5.

3. The "Letter to Hans Luther" of November 21, 1521, can be found in *Luther's Works* (American Edition), vol. 48, p. 336.

4. "On the Councils and the Church," Part III (1539), in Lull, ed., *Martin Luther's Basic Theological Writings*, p. 551.

5. Søren Kierkegaard (1813–55) attempted to restore depth and truth to the theology and church life of his time. His critique of the Danish State (Lutheran) Church in his last years is found in *Attack upon Christendom* (Princeton, N.J., 1944). He reflected frequently on what a different task Luther would face if he were to return, after the centuries that had passed, to a very changed context.

6. "Preface to the Wittenberg Edition" (1539), in Lull, ed., *Martin Luther's Basic Theological Writings*, pp. 67–68.

Chapter 2

1. The book in question was Brevard Childs, *Biblical Theology of the Old and New Testaments* (Minneapolis: Fortress, 1992). The book contains one of the best available discussions of Luther as an interpreter of Scripture, pp. 43–47.

2. See "Preface to the New Testament" (1522), in Lull, ed., *Martin Luther's Basic Theological Writings*, p. 117, in which Luther argues that James's epistle is one of "straw" with "nothing of the gospel" in it.

3. For Luther's early lectures on Romans, see *Luther's Works*, vol. 25 (Concordia Publishing House), or *Lectures on Romans* in the Library of Christian Classics (Westminster: John Knox). The late work, "On the Jews and Their Lies," can be found in volume 47 of *Luther's Works* (Fortress Press).

4. Luther's *The Freedom of a Christian* (1520), one of his greatest writings, was (on the advice of those still seeking to make peace) submitted to Pope Leo X with an introductory letter in which Luther claimed that he "had spoken only good and honorable words" concerning the prelate—which is quite a remarkable statement to make in 1520. See Lull, ed., *Martin Luther's Basic Theological Writings*, p. 586.

5. Selections can be found in *Martin Luther's Basic Theological Writings*, pp. 173–226. For the whole text of Luther's response to Erasmus's attack on him, see *Luther's Works*, vol. 33.

6. See Luther's "Lectures on Galatians" (1519) and (1535) in *Luther's Works*, vols. 26–27.

7. Nicholas von Amsdorf (1483–1565), another close friend of Luther's and a leader of the hard-line Lutheran party after Luther's death, became bishop of Naumberg in 1542 and continued there, with difficulty, until the emperor's troops captured the territory in 1547. He was a nephew of Staupitz, Luther's superior in the Augustinian order. Family connections seem not to have hurt in those days either.

8. Lutherans have often been quite caustic about the part played by Anglicans in the divorce of Henry VIII (1533) without paying much attention to the parallels in the roles played by Luther, Melanchthon, and Bucer in condoning the bigamy of Philip of Hesse (1540). See Martin Brecht, *Martin Luther: The Preservation of the Church* (Minneapolis: Fortress, 1993), pp. 205–15.

9. See Martin Brecht, *Martin Luther: His Road to Reformation* (Minneapolis: Fortress, 1985), p. 111. The woman's name was Anna Weller of Molsdorf.

10. Martin Luther, "Meditation concerning Christ's Passion" (1519) in *Martin Luther's Basic Theological Works*, p. 171.

Chapter 3

1. Thus I learned that Luther apparently used his new heavenly knowledge of English not only to read Shakespeare, but also Charles Dickens. See chapter 1 for his interest in *Hamlet*.

2. Luther often slipped in a German word or two, I suppose when he thought that I might understand. I have largely spared the reader from these—but that "nein" or "no" is too deep in my memory to omit.

3. By an interesting set of circumstances, Luther died in the town where he was born—Eisleben—just having settled a long dispute about the local aristocracy.

4. I would like to know who told Luther that he missed a lot in Rome. Among the possibilities are Leo X (see chapter 2), Bonhoeffer (see chapter 5), or Johann Wolfgang von Goethe (1749–1832), the German poet and dramatist with whose *Faust* Luther seems to be familiar (see the hint in chapter 3).

5. Luther entered the Augustinian order (more precisely, the Reformed Order of Augustinian friars) in Erfurt in the summer of 1505. The next year, he took the vows of a monk and prepared for priestly ordination (not all monks were ordained), and eventually was assigned to study theology, especially the Bible.

6. Throughout his life, Luther was a strong advocate for public education for boys and girls, and a defender of the need to study not only the Bible, but also the great classics, especially those Greek and Latin authors that he had loved from his own schooling. He felt they were in some ways even more helpful than the Scriptures for knowing how to live in this world. See "To the Councilmen of All Cities in Germany That They Establish and Maintain Christian Schools" (1524), in Lull, ed., *Martin Luther's Basic Theological Writings*, pp. 733–34.

7. Andreas Carlstadt (ca.1480–1541) was initially Luther's senior faculty colleague at Wittenberg. They debated Eck together at Leipzig in 1519. During Luther's absence at the Wartburg Castle, Carlstadt assumed leadership of the Reformation in Wittenberg and began to make radical changes. At Christmas 1521 he offered the Mass in both kinds and in the language of the people. He was also among the first of the clergy to marry. Luther blamed him for the ensuing turmoil and their relations continued to be difficult until Carlstadt left Saxony for good. He went to Switzerland and became a professor at Basel.

8. Martin Chemnitz (1522–86) was the greatest Lutheran theologian of the generation after Luther's death, remembered for his learned and critical commentaries on the Council of Trent and his attempt to reunite the two factions of Lutherans who had been feuding since Luther's death. This was accomplished chiefly by a document called the "Formula of Concord" (1577), and by assembling the key Lutheran teachings into a collection called *The Book of Concord* (1580).

9. Jan Hus or Huss (ca.1369–1415) was a professor at the University of Prague who preached in the language of the people (Czech) and criticized corruption in the church. In the end, his writings led to his being ordered to appear at the Council of Constance, where he was—despite a safe-conduct from the authorities—burned at the stake. Luther seemed to many in his day to be a "new Hus," but since the earlier figure had been condemned as a heretic, it was not a compliment when Eck made the comparison.

10. Philipp Melanchthon (1497–1560) was Luther's brilliant younger colleague and most important coworker. The men remained close despite some tensions—as much temperamental as theological—between them. Because Luther could not, as a condemned heretic, come into the presence of the emperor, Melanchthon was the major drafter and then presenter of the *Augsburg Confession* in 1530.

11. Luther's health problems late in life included kidney stones so severe that he almost died from being unable to urinate, and later, heart failure. Details are well summarized in Mark U. Edwards Jr., *Luther's Last Battles* (Ithaca, N.Y.: Cornell University Press, 1983), chapter 1. Edwards argues convincingly for Luther's continuing productivity as a writer despite illness and discouragement.

12. A bull is a written document from a pope on a serious important matter, the name coming from the Latin *bulla* for "seal," referring to the special way in which the documents were authenticated. Leo X issued "Exsurge Domine" warning Luther that he must recant on June 15, 1520, and the second, "Decet Romanum Pontificem" on January 3, 1521, which excommunicated him.

13. The story might be "Earth's Holocaust" by Nathaniel Hawthorne—a quite amazing nineteenth-century prediction of things to come in our own century. It can be found in many paperback collections of Hawthorne stories and definitively in Nathaniel Hawthorne, *Tales and Sketches* (New York: Library of America, 1982), pp. 887–906.

14. Diet comes closest to our English word Parliament, although with more limited legislative authority. One was held annually in Germany with the emperor himself often in attendance. Luther's prince Frederick the Wise, Elector of Saxony, was an important person in this gathering that included not only various secular rulers, but also prince-bishops who had great authority over parts of Germany, including such great cities as Cologne, Mainz, Trier, Bamberg, and Wurzburg.

15. By "the world" Luther means the world that he knew—Europe, although in Charles's case that also included much of the "New World," which was under his domain as King of Spain. It is more complex to determine who was the most powerful person in the whole world at that time, if one includes the great kingdoms of Asia.

16. See Ernest G. Schwiebert, *The Reformation* (Minneapolis: Fortress, 1996), p. 181.

17. These were hemorrhoids and constipation among other things, as the many letters to friends written in his ten months in the Wartburg make quite clear. See *Luther's Works*, vol. 48.

18. Martin Luther, "Letter to Philipp Melanchthon of May 26, 1521," in *Luther's Works*, vol. 48, p. 232.

Chapter 4

1. See Martin Luther, "On the Councils and the Church," Part III (1539), in Lull, ed., *Martin Luther's Basic Theological Writings*, p. 550.

2. For this material, see "Eight Sermons in Wittenberg" (1522), in, *Martin Luther's Basic Theological Writings*, pp. 414–44. Luther had been condemned by Charles V, the Holy Roman Emperor, at the Diet of Worms the previous April. He lived the rest of his life under that death sentence, which could have been carried out at any point.

3. Frederick, who supported Luther without endorsing the Reformation, on his deathbed received the sacrament from his chaplain, George Spalatin, in both kinds—that is the bread and the wine, which had become an identifier of those supporting the Reformation, as the Roman church continued to insist that the laity should receive only the bread. Spalatin (1484–1545) was a contemporary and eventually friend

of Luther's, a humanist scholar who served as the major adviser to Frederick the Wise. He had been ordained in 1508. For a fine description of the rule and politics of Frederick, see Ernest G. Schwiebert, *The Reformation* (Minneapolis: Fortress, 1996), chapter 14.

4. The Elector John gave the Luthers the former Augustinian monastery as a wedding present. It was a wonderful and terrible gift. See chapter 6 for Katie's problems in managing the Luther household. The noble visitors included Electress Elizabeth of Brandenburg (separated from her husband) and also her daughter, Princess Margaret of Anhalt. See Martin Brecht, *Martin Luther: The Preservation of the Church* (Minneapolis: Fortress, 1993), chapter 9.

5. See "Sermon on the Estate of Marriage" (1519) in *Martin Luther's Basic Theological Writings*, pp. 630–37.

6. Luther's daughter Magdalena died at age 13 in 1542. It was a grief from which the Luthers never really recovered, in some ways the beginning of the last hard chapter of his life story.

7. See "Smalcald Articles" (1537) in *Martin Luther's Basic Theological Writings*, p. 527.

8. Dietrich Bonhoeffer (1906–45) was one of the great theologians of the twentieth century both in his interest in authentic discipleship and the form of Christian community, and in his witness against Hitler during the German church struggle. For "cheap grace," see Dietrich Bonhoeffer, *The Cost of Discipleship* (Macmillan: New York, 1959). For more on Luther and Bonhoeffer, see chapter 5.

9. "Lectures on Galatians" (1519), in *Luther's Works*, vol. 27, pp. 346–48.

10. Martin Luther, "Whether One May Flee from a Deadly Plague" (1527), in *Martin Luther's Basic Theological Writings*, pp. 736–55.

11. Ibid., pp. 747–48.

12. "The Blessed Sacrament of the Body and Blood of Christ and the Brotherhoods" (1519), in *Martin Luther's Basic Theological Writings*, p. 247.

13. See chapter 1.

14. "Small Catechism" (1528), in *Martin Luther's Basic Theological Writings*, pp. 480–81. The wording in the text is slightly different from the way I spoke it from memory.

15. For the letter, see *Luther's Works*, vol. 50, pp. 273–81. For background on the whole incident, see Brecht, *Martin Luther: The Preservation of the Church*, pp. 262–65.

16. See Brecht, chapter 14, for a detailed account of Luther's death and burial.

17. See chapter 6 for details about why this happened.

18. "Last Sermon in Wittenberg" (1546), in *Luther's Works*, vol. 51, p. 373.

Chapter 5

1. It was, in fact, the choir and orchestra of Augustana Lutheran Church of Denver, Colorado.

2. The best serious treatment of this painful and complex topic is Heiko Oberman, *The Roots of Anti-Semitism* (Philadelphia: Fortress, 1984).

3. Martin Luther, "Against the Robbing and Murdering Hordes of Peasants" (1525), in *Luther's Works*, vol. 46 (Philadelphia: Fortress, 1967), p. 54.

4. "That Jesus Christ Was Born a Jew" (1523), in *Luther's Works*, vol. 45 (Philadelphia: Fortress, 1962), pp. 197–229.

5. "On the Jews and Their Lies" (1543), in *Luther's Works*, vol. 47 (Philadelphia: Fortress, 1971), pp. 137–305. For an example of the letters, see "To Mrs. Martin Luther" (February 7, 1546), in *Luther's Works*, vol. 50 (Philadelphia: Fortress, 1975), pp. 301–4.

6. I felt in retrospect that Luther must have called him "your Shakespeare" because he wrote in English.

7. See letters to Katherine von Bora Luther in which he complains that the rulers of Mansfeld are not proceeding vigorously enough to expel the Jews from their territory (*Luther's Works*, vol. 50, pp. 302–3).

8. "Two Sermons in Weimar" (1522), in *Luther's Works*, vol. 51 (Philadelphia: Fortress, 1959), pp. 103–17.

9. I must admit I also always think of the cry of certain Jews in the passion account according to Saint Matthew: "His blood be upon us and on our children" (Matt. 27:25). This has been the source of so much justification of Christian hatred of Jews that it is hard to recover a positive image for blood falling on the head.

10. A dragon or—more precisely—a winged serpent was the signature symbol of Lucas Cranach the Elder. It appears in a tiny form on most of his paintings after 1508, the year in which Frederick the Wise made him a member of the nobility with this symbol on his coat of arms.

Chapter 6

1. What should we make of Katherine's offering two names? It may be that either was acceptable to her. But since Amsdorf never married and was seen by many to be a confirmed bachelor, it may have been a very diplomatic way to say that, if she married anyone, it would be Luther.

Amsdorf's bachelor status was one of the reasons that he was later named the first Lutheran bishop—in Naumberg. It was thought that an unmarried bishop—even if an Evangelical—might be more acceptable to the cathedral chapter. See Martin Brecht, *Martin Luther: The Preservation of the Church* (Minneapolis: Fortress, 1993), pp. 300–308.

2. In the customs of that period, the betrothal was the beginning of living together; the marriage followed at a convenient time for those who had to travel. The details of the betrothal are rather startling to contemporary attitudes. See Martin Brecht, *Martin Luther: Shaping and Defining the Reformation* (Minneapolis: Fortress, 1990), pp. 197–201.